D1580258

WRITE LANGUAGE

The New Secrets of Writing
Letters that Really Work.

WRITE LANGUAGE

The New Secrets of Writing Letters that Really Work

Allan Pease
Paul Dunn

© Allan Pease & Paul Dunn 1988

All rights reserved. No part of this publication may be reproduced or transmitted in any form or by any means without prior permission from the publishers.

First published in 1998 by Pease Training Corporation and
The Results Corporation as a joint-venture.

Pease International, P.O. Box 1260, Buderim, QLD 4556, Australia
Tel: + 61 7 5445 5600 Fax: + 61 7 5445 5688
info@peaseinternational.com
www.peaseinternational.com

National Library of Australia
Catalogue-in-Publication data
Pease Allan, Dunn Paul
Write Language
ISBN 1 9208160 0 3
Reprinted 1992, 1995, 1996, 2003

1. Written Communication (Psychology)

Edited by Allan Pease, Paul Dunn, Desley Truscott
Illustrated by John Hepworth
Cover Design by Tiffany Cruickshank, Trovato Design
Printed by McPhersons Printing Group, Australia
A Tale of Two Cities by Charles Dickens

Distributed in Australia and New Zealand by HarperCollins Publishers Pty Ltd
Distributed in Asia by STP Books Distributors
Distributed in Hong Kong by Publishers Association Ltd
Distributed in South Africa by Oxford University Press

Contents

'Of all those arts in which the wise excel
Nature's chief masterpiece is writing well'

Introduction

Congratulations.

You've just taken a very positive step towards dramatically improving your communication with others.
And we do mean dramatically.

People like you who've invested in **WRITE LANGUAGE** *and put the ideas to work* have reported amazing gains. Like the Travel Agent who generated an additional $1.5 million in bookings in less than 4 weeks.

Like the photographer who rang excitedly to tell about the $3000 job he got that, as he put it . . .'I could not have done it without **WRITE LANGUAGE**'.

Like the woman who got the job she just didn't expect to get. And the young man who got a date he thought he'd never get.

You'll see how to make gains like these too. But only when you *use* the skills. To make that a certainty for you, you'll see that **WRITE LANGUAGE** is set out in a very special way.

Let's take a quick look at the book so that you can discover exactly how to use it.

The first 2 Chapters are critical. Read and understand them thoroughly because they form the basis of the entire book. In fact, you'll find you may need to keep coming back to these key Chapters—that's how important they are.

Then, as you move through Chapters 3 to 7, you'll find some brilliant new ideas, many specific skills and techniques for building almost any letter you want to write.

You'll see why the opening of your letters is so important. And you'll find how to create ideas that let the *real* you come through.

Together we'll show you ideas and 'grass roots' skills that make your letters come alive for your reader so that they feel you're in the room talking with them.

And then in Chapter 7 you'll see how to close your letters to get the *action* you want.

Again, you'll find yourself going back to these Chapters time and time again as you develop and refine the skills. After a while, you and even you closest friends will find it difficult to believe that you're writing letters that are so effective. But let's get back to our tour of the book.

In Chapters 8, 9 and 10 we start to add icing to the cake and cream to your coffee. Here you'll see some special purpose letters that illustrate how you can use the techniques to improve your result.

But a word of caution!

Please don't go to these Chapters until you've read and understood (and used) the ideas in Chapters 1-7. To do so is counter-productive because you'll be running the risk of missing some very important concepts from these early Chapters.

Chapter 11 is about a very important person—you. Here you'll find out how to put your own personal touch into each letter you write so that the ideas become yours, not ours.

When that happens, we will have communicated in a special way. You'll start achieving much more. And your reader will think of you as 'different'.

Before you begin your journey through **WRITE LANGUAGE** we'd like you to know something of the pleasure we had writing this book. We believe it's a contribution to making human communication much more effective.

But that pleasure didn't stop when **WRITE LANGUAGE** was finally printed. The pleasure continues as people like you use the skills and tell us about the results they get.

Even though e-mail has become the modern form of written communication it makes no difference to the art of effective letter writing as e-mail is nothing more than an electronic postal delivery. Whether you send your correspondence on an e-mail page or by an attachment letter the principles revealed here hold true.

Interestingly, the avalanche of e-mails now sent to us makes it more interesting to receive and send a real letter!

Even the humble 'P.S.' has almost disappeared from correspondence now. It was originally used to show an afterthought but, because of computers, is no longer necessary. But, as you'll see in Chapter 6, it's still a powerful thing to include in any letter, including e-mail.

Write and tell us of your success. Enjoy **WRITE LANGUAGE** and above all, continue to enjoy…

… good things

ALLAN PEASE & PAUL DUNN

P.S. For the sake of simplicity note that throughout **WRITE LANGUAGE** the word 'he' is generic. It can mean 'he' or 'she' (or ít').

About the Examples

You'll find **WRITE LANGUAGE** has many examples in it to help you understand and use each key idea.

In researching the book it was easy to get examples of bad letters (we get them everyday) but not so easy to find good ones.

So, you'll notice that some of the examples come from Paul and Allan's own experience and from their own businesses.

But you'll find them easy to relate to and easy to 'translate' into your business and personal life.

To find out a little more about training programmes, books and Seminars by Paul and Allan, you'll see we've included some special pages for you right at the back of the book.

One

How to Think 'Outside the Box'

Many people love puzzles.

Maybe you're one of them. Maybe even the dictionary has one of those strange sounding names ending in 'ic' or 'ac' that describes a puzzle-lover.

So if you're a 'puzzliac' you'll enjoy this puzzle. It's called the 9 Dot Puzzle.

It shows how we tend to confine ourselves within a rigid framework—even though that framework isn't rigid at all.

And it shows us how we impose rules on ourselves that weren't imposed by the problem—we just imagine that the rules are imposed on us.

Here's the 9 Dots puzzle. You have 9 dots arranged in a square like this:

    •   •   •

    •   •   •

    •   •   •

Begin by putting your pencil on any dot and, *without taking your pencil from the paper, draw 4 straight and connected lines* without going back over any previous lines so that your pencil (or the lines it's drawn) pass through every dot.

Most attempts look like this:

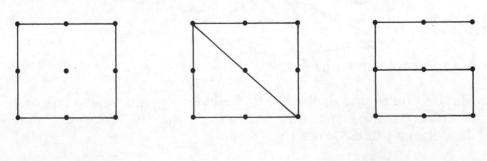

missed a dot   5 lines   non-connected or

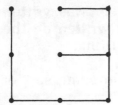

tracking back

These attempts at solutions all try to solve the problem by staying within the confines of the 9 dots—that is, staying within the box.

To solve the 9 Dot problem (and to solve many other problems too) we need to think 'outside the box'.

When you do that the solution comes a lot easier. It looks like this:

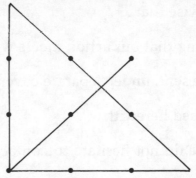

And so it is with writing letters.

You see, when we're actually talking with someone one-on-one, face-to-face, there really is no 'box'. We say more or less whatever we like as long as we're prepared to take the consequences.

Yet when we sit down to write a letter several things may happen:

* our mind goes blank
* we start thinking 'This is a letter. I'm not good at writing creative letters'
or, * we start thinking 'This is a letter. I remember what the How to Write Better Business Letters course I did at school said I must do. I'll do it that way'.

The trouble is that the book the course was based on was written in the 19th century. And not only that, it was written on the *presumption* that you had to be formal in letter writing.

So, when you write letters, you put yourself in some sort of mental box.

And when you do that your letters don't work well for you. Worst of all, they're not 'you'.

We see it every day when we see letters that use words and phrases like this:

> '. . . enclosed please find our brochure for your perusal'

> '. . . assuring you of our best attention at all times'

> '. . . we refer to your letter of the 6 instant and wish to advise that . . .'

> '. . . trusting that our action meets with your approval'

> '. . . we've sent, under separate cover, . . .'

> '. . . enclosed herewith . . .'

> '. . . please do not hesitate to contact the undersigned . . .'

> '. . . enclosed as per your request . . .'

> '. . . pursuant to our discussion . . .'

> '. . . we acknowledge receipt of your correspondence as of the above date . . .'

Can you imagine talking with someone in business and saying to them 'herewith is our brochure for your perusal!' Imagine if you got the reply, 'Well thank you sir, I remain your trusted servant'.

So clearly, change is needed. But that doesn't mean you need to change your personality. You're O.K.

What you need is to find ways of projecting who you really are to those who read your letters.

Also, we're now in an age where the building of personal relationships is more important in business and personal life than the stiff, starchy formality of yesteryear.

So, it's our 'style' that needs to change so that we can break out of that restrictive mental box.

And that's precisely what we'll be doing here.

To start that process let's look at some of the supposed 'rules' of letter writing and encourage you to break free of those rules.

The Old Rules	The New Rules
Always be grammatically correct	Tell it like it is
For example: Never use a preposition with which to end a sentence	As Winston Churchill once wrote: "this is the sort of stuff up with which I will not put'.
Never begin a sentence with 'and' or 'but'	Write the way you talk Begin sentences with 'And' and 'But' if it carries the reader along. And not only that, recognise that doing that can add impact to a point.
A sentence must have a verb, object and subject	Untrue. Short, one word 'sentences' are very powerful. You can change to this new

Style today. Right
now and be amazed
with the Results.

You'll see these and many more supposed 'rules' broken in many of the example letters in this book. Not because it's necessarily good to break rules. But because the test of a good letter is the answer to this question:

Did the letter achieve the result you wanted?

And that means:

Did you break through the clutter?

Did you break through the clutter caused by all the other letters your reader received today? Did he have 6 letters (that's another 'rule' we've broken about numbers, isn't it?) – 6 letters demanding money and yours got put on the bottom of the stack?

Did he get 13 e-mails today asking him to invest time and/or money in some new product or idea? And 9 more offering Viagra or re-finance? And yours happened to be the 14th one opened and then he discarded it saying 'All this damn junk mail!'

Clearly, one way to get through that clutter is to be different.

Now that *doesn't* mean breaking the rules so that you'll be different. What we're suggesting is this. **You'll be different just by being yourself** – the normal you who talks with people one-on-one.

So you can be prepared for this. To apply the rules in **WRITE LANGUAGE** you're going to have to un-learn some of the old restrictive and formal ideas so that you can make way for the new ones.

It will be a valuable experience for you because when you learn the concepts and skills in this book that get you outside the box, your letters will start to work for you like never before.

When you grasp hold of the ideas in the next Chapter and use those ideas as the base for all your letters, you'll be amazed at how effective your letters will be.

We'll get to that once we've had a quick look at some don'ts and do's—or more precisely, once we've had a look at some words to avoid and some words to use.

Avoid These	Use These
Herewith	You'll see I've attached your . . .
Commence	Get underway, start
Ascertain	Discover, find out, you'll see
Acquire	When you use, when you own, get
Endeavour	Will
Expeditious	Quick
Facilitate	Make it easier for you
In the event of	If
In order to	So, so that you'll
With regard to	About
Prior to	Before
Due to the fact that	Because
In the amount of	For
Cost	Investment
Contract	Paperwork, agreement

The words and phrases in the 'use' list are far less formal. You'll notice too that they can form the basis of more powerful, easy-to-read phrases.

Using them (and many more phrases you'll discover soon) will give your letters that 'me-to-you' or personal touch. And that's a touch that will make your letters so much more effective.

Effectiveness and being yourself is what **WRITE LANGUAGE** is about. Thinking outside the box is crucial. And so is learning about a new radio station in the next Chapter. That is. . . . .

Two

A New Radio Station for You

Next time you sit down with pen poised ready to write a letter, get a picture of your reader in your mind.

And think of him sitting there looking almost like a visitor from some far off planet. He's got no eyes and no ears. He's got just one of those spiral T.V. antennae sticking out of where his ears would normally be.

This antenna is tuned to a very special and very selective frequency. It's so selective that if the message you broadcast is not on that frequency, the message will fall on deaf ears.

Or, to put that in letter-writing terms, if the message you write is not on the right wavelength, (the other person's wavelength) the message will not be understood or acted upon. It will go the way of many letters . . . right into the WPB*.

Fortunately, the wavelength or frequency that your reader is tuned to is fairly predictable. And that frequency has a name. It's WII-FM.

That's right. Your reader is tuned into a radio station called WII-FM.

And it's call sign?

WHAT'S IN IT—FOR ME

This means that your reader is reading each line with a WII-FM filter between his eyes and his brain.

In simple terms then, anything that's on the right WII-FM frequency gets accepted it gets through the filter. Anything that's not on WII-FM gets rejected (I say 'in simple terms' because there are other ways of getting through the eye-to-brain filter as you'll discover soon).

Now what we've covered so far seems simple enough doesn't it? And it makes sense. Yet it's amazing how we get it wrong.

Take a look at this typical piece of direct mail I received as I was writing this Chapter and then we'll analyse it. (You'll notice names have been removed to protect the guilty.)

*WPB—WASTE PAPER BASKET (I only did this to show you the power of an asterisk in letters. I bet you read WPB and then came right down to read this. There's a lesson in that. We'll discuss it in depth later on.)

XYZ COMPANY AUSTRALIA LIMITED CORDIALLY
INVITES YOU TO A SPECIAL PREVIEW OF
THE NEW:

740 T

ANAMORPHIC ZOOM COLOUR COPIER

&

AB40

PERSONAL COPIER

TO BE HELD AT:

THE RIVER ROOM

STEWARTS HAMILTON HOTEL

KINGSFORD SMITH DRIVE

HAMILTON QLD.

ON:

TUESDAY 2ND & WEDNESDAY 3RD SEPTEMBER

ALSO ON DISPLAY WILL BE:

**THE LATEST IN MICROFILM AND PLAN
PRINTING EQUIPMENT**

TO CONFIRM YOUR ATTENDANCE, OR TO
SIMPLY REQUEST MORE INFORMATION,
WOULD YOU PLEASE CONTACT THE WRITER
ON XXX-XXXX.

Yours faithfully,

XYZ COMPANY AUSTRALIA LIMITED.

I did say typical didn't I?

Where is the WII-FM? Just what is in it for me?

I'm sure the person who wrote the letter is genuinely excited about the 740T . . . but I'm not. And equally, the 'anamorphic zoom' probably makes the letter writer foam at the mouth. But it leaves the letter reader cold.

And what did you think of the last line?

> . . . would you please contact **the writer** on XXX-XXXX'

This is an example of the starchiness and rigid formality that we've been taught. It's an example of being bound by rules—rules written last century.

We write phrases like this in letters because, until now, we've been taught to think inside the box. Because, until now, we've been bound by those habit patterns from years of being taught to conform. Yet those habit patterns we've built up are so damn ineffective aren't they?

Take this next letter for example. Check how impersonal and ineffective it is.

Dear Sir/Madam,
RE: STAFF DEVELOPMENT AND TRAINING PROGRAMS

Further to our recent telephone communication with your company, we have pleasure in enclosing our brochure for your perusal.

As your Company is aware, training and development of personnel plays a vital role in the success of a company's operation. The enclosed information highlights the courses available which could be suitable to your needs by providing an alternative training to your existing programs.

Please call for an appointment to inspect our in-house training facilities, or we can arrange to call and see you should you wish to obtain further information on course content and availability.

Yours faithfully,

Hopeless isn't it?

It begins with a vague cliche:

> 'Further to our recent communication with your
>   company . . .'

In effect they're saying, 'we didn't speak with you, we spoke
with your company'.

The reader feels neglected. It's as if we're saying we're not
interested in him, we're only interested in the company.

But it gets worse. The second paragraph begins this way:

> 'As your company is aware. . .'

It's like saying, 'Your company is aware **but you're not!**'

Impersonal. Amateurish. Ineffective. And almost insulting. It's
those old habit patterns at work again.

Now let's find a better way.

And that better way starts by remembering to think outside
the box and by thinking in WII-FM terms.

To drive the point home for you, let's look at another example
where WII-FM is completely ignored by the letter writer. And
so the letter gets completely ignored by the reader.

Dear Sir,

If your Company is in the business of giving advice about computer related solutions for importing, warehousing and distribution, merchandising or manufacturing—please read on.

Our Company is planning a series of Presentations at the Sheraton Hotel on 3rd and 4th September. Attendance is by invitation only, and is designed specifically for persons who regularly advise their clients in such matters. The Presentations are the same on each day, in order that you can choose which day is convenient for you.

If you wish to attend, please call Robyn Donovan on XXXXXXX so we can send you a formal invitation.

Yours faithfully,

John Smith.

How many people would you think they got to the Sheraton in September?

They expected 300 responses. They got 5. Why?

Because there is no WII-FM. What's in it for me if I go to the Seminar? What will I get out of it?

Sure. It's a nice enough letter. But all it achieves is minimal response.

Well here's the good news. If you write letters that look anything like that, you're about to find out how easy it is to change. You're about to discover how to write effective letters. You'll find out how easy it is to get the result you want.

You see, in the letters you've seen so far in this Chapter, the people writing them are missing one simple thing. They're missing the first letter-writing Power Point. Here it is:

POWER POINT 1

ALWAYS TELL THE READER,

IN SPECIFIC TERMS,

EXACTLY WHAT HE'LL GET,

FIND OUT,

DISCOVER OR BE ABLE TO ACHIEVE

WHEN HE TAKES THE ACTION

YOU WANT HIM TO TAKE.

In other words, when you're writing letters remember that your reader has his antenna tuned to WII-FM.
You see, when you do that, you'll discover something interesting. You'll find you'll start using words like I've just used in that previous sentence. (Check the number of 'you's' in it.)

When you think WII-FM, you'll automatically use words that keep your reader involved. You'll build sentences that talk in WII-FM terms.

Here's an example—a letter written to Paul's clients who use his Incoming Call Telephone Programme called 'Phone Right'. This letter tells them, in WII-FM terms, all about an additional programme dealing with making Outgoing Calls. Read on . . .

Good morning Sheryl,

It's delightful to have you as one of our newer 'Phone Right' clients.

Thank you for becoming our client and congratulations once again on recognising how important the telephone is to your business.

Thanks too for asking for more information on the Outgoing *Call part of the programme. We call it 'Phone Right—Part 2.'*

> *Here's a quick outline of just some of what you'll find in Part 2.*

In simple terms, you'll discover how your telephone can be used both to save *you a great deal of money and time. And you'll find out too how you can use your telephone to* sell more *of your products and services. Let's look quickly at the 'savings' part Sheryl.*

If you have any slow payers in your business, you'll get some terrific new ideas on how to collect money from them—quickly and simply. Just by using some new techniques that work without *threats or high pressure.*

For example, one Perth businessman, to his absolute astonishment, collected $15,000 on his first try . . . and he was almost prepared to write it off! The programme shows you exactly how to do it.

But perhaps the biggest gain occurs by using those new techniques to create new customers. *New customers who add new profits and new opportunities for you.*

As you listen to 'Phone Right—Part 2' you'll find out exactly how to get face-to-face with people who need your products and services. You'll see how simple it is to make appointments (even with 'difficult' prospective clients) . . . once you know and use the techniques we go through in the programme.

You'll see exactly how to design and write effective sales letters *to make it even easier for you to get together with people who are not yet your customers.*

It really is powerful and extremely effective stuff. For example, Julie Cox of Colonial Mutual in Melbourne had what she describes as 'six blank weeks'. Then by using the techniques she jumped to $1700 commission in the first week. And she hasn't looked back since. You can get that same kind of result.

And objections? Never again will they be a problem for you on the phone. You'll get a terrific 1-2-3 step plan to deal effectively with any objection you receive on the phone. You'll find you can even use these ideas to add to the skills you've already picked up from Part 1 of the programme.

But that's not all you'll get.

Like your existing Phone Right programme, Part 2 goes into detail and into specific 'nitty-gritty' areas. Again we use simulated phone calls to show you exactly how the new skills you'll learn can be used to increase your business. It's done not with pressure but with a new customer-oriented focus. And it's done with an approach that puts the other person first.

For example, you'll hear the exact techniques and words you need to handle the secretary or receptionist who refuses to put you through to her boss until she's interrogated you like you're a Secret Service Agent.

And one entire section of this profit building programme deals in quite a unique way with the subject called **TELEMARKETING***—how to use your phone to sell your products and services without a face-to-face visit. In fact, in this section you'll hear not simulated phone calls but an actual* **live** *one as we show you exactly how it's done—exactly how you can build additional sales.*
Phone Right Part 2 has so much in it that: a) it's a full 4 hour programme and, b) it's taken me quite a few words to tell you just a little bit about it.

So . . . maybe you deserve a reward for reading this far and for acting on what you've read.

Let me explain that to you now . . .

There's quite a difference isn't there? And that difference comes from thinking in WII-FM terms. Once you do that, you'll find your written communication takes on a whole new dimension for you *and* your reader.

We'll talk more about this idea in Chapter 5. For now though, and to make it easy for you to think *and write* in WII-FM terms, here's a neat little table for you. It's designed specifically to make it easier for you to remember *and* use the key ideas in this Chapter. That way, your letters and your ideas will really come to life for you *and* your readers.

By using this table, you'll see how all of a sudden your reader becomes involved in your letter. He's nodding. He's thinking, 'that makes sense'. Your ideas have 'come alive' in his mind. He's painting pictures of the results he can achieve by actually using your product or service. And *that* is exciting.

You'll see in the table how WII-FM phrases can be used at the beginning of sentences—we call them 'Openers'.

And you'll notice too how some WII-FM phrases can be used in the middle of sentences to 'translate' the key ideas into the reader's language—to make your ideas come alive. We call these phrases 'Translators'.

OPENERS*	AS IN . . .
You see . . .	You see, John, when you see our new anamorphic zoom in action, you'll realise exactly why it will have such significant effect on the quality of copies you produce.
You'll see . . .	You'll see precisely how the new computer technology will help you save . . .
You'll discover . . .	You'll discover an amazingly simple truth about . . .
You'll find . . .	You'll find it brilliantly simple to use . . .
You'll recognise . . .	You'll recognise just how valuable . . .

*'Openers' are typically used at the beginning of sentences and/or paragraphs.

You'll hear . . .	You'll hear, perhaps for the first time, how . . .
You'll be able to see at first hand. . .	You'll be able to see at first hand exactly how using the new idea will . . .
You'll realise . . .	You'll realise just how effective . . .

TRANSLATORS****

So. . .	It has a dual processor so speed is doubled
What this means is . . .	What this means to you is a significant increase in effectiveness and productivity
And, as importantly. . .	And, as importantly, the freedom to assign work much more flexibly
So that you . . .	You'll see just how solid the new furniture is so that you can considerably reduce maintenance costs
So you . . .	That's $94 including unlimited kilometres so you can travel as far as you like without adding in extra dollars

The concept of WII-FM really is crucial. It means practicing EMPATHY. It means getting into the other person's shoes, thinking like they think, seeing things the way *they* see them.

Whenever I think of seeing things the way other people see them, I think of the story of Frank Johnson.

Picture the scene.

It is the meeting of the Sales and Marketing Executives (known as 'SAMMY') Club in San Francisco.

This is their big meeting of the year—the one where they announce the 'Salesperson of the Year'.

***'Translators' translate key product features into benefits for the reader. They take something like 'anamorphic zoom' and put it into WII-FM terms *so that* the idea really comes alive in the reader's mind. You'll discover more about these 'translators' in Chapter 5.

The ballroom is packed with 3000 people. At 9 o'clock the chairman gets up, taps the microphone and begins . . .

'Ladies and Gentlemen, this is the moment we've all been waiting for. The moment when we announce the winner of the Salesperson of the Year Award.'

The crowd claps anxiously. The chairman waves his hands to keep the crowd quiet.

He continues:

'Do we have any people in the audience from the great profession of Real Estate selling?'

Hundreds of hands go up.

'Then you in particular are going to be thrilled this evening. Because the award this year is to a member of your industry'.

The Real Estate people cheer loudly.

'And the person . . .' continues the Chairman, '. . . earned $12,000.'

A hush descends. Does he mean $12,000 per week, per day, per month or what? The Chairman leans on the lectern,

'$12,000 in this past year.'

The hush is now a stunned silence. They're thinking, '$12,000 a year! But *everyone* in this room earns far more than that!'

Many in the crowd think that the Chairman's had one drink too many. You can hear a pin drop as the Chairman says,

'Ladies and Gentlemen, the SAMMY Salesperson of the Year is . . . Frank Johnson'

The spotlight picks up Frank Johnson in the audience to the Chairman's right. They notice something a little strange about Frank Johnson. He's fumbling around. He doesn't spring to his feet and rush to the stage. He doesn't really look like a confident salesperson.

And then the Chairman's voice sorts out the confusion . . .

'And as you can see, Frank Johnson is totally blind.'

The audience is stunned. Together they rise as Frank Johnson, a *blind* Real Estate salesperson is ushered to the stage.

The applause dies down. The Chairman hands Frank Johnson his Award and asks him . . .

'Frank, how do you deal with your disability—how on earth can a blind person sell Real Estate?'

Frank Johnson replies . . .

'Disability? I don't have a disability at all. I think I have an advantage over you sighted folk. You see, when I sell, I'm forced to sell through other people's eyes. And not only that, my prospects always have to drive *me* back to the office! I'm forced to sell through other people's eyes'.

That is EMPATHY. *That* is WII-FM. Seeing things as other people see them.

It means that a vital skill for you to develop is the skill of writing words and picturing your reader reading them.

So with that story about Frank Johnson and the examples we've looked at, you now have a good grasp of WII-FM. Let's move on and discover what many people regard as the most difficult part of a letter. It's called . . .

Three

How to Grab Your Reader Early—The Opening

This is it.

The part of the book that will make you say 'I'm glad I invested in this.'

You see, have you ever stared at a blank piece of paper and wished that **SOMETHING** in fact **ANYTHING** would come into your head? But nothing did.

You have?

Then we're on the same wavelength.

Because I've been there a hundred times.

Openings can be hard can't they? But you've just seen some techniques that make them much more effective. We'll go through those techniques in a while but first let's give you Power Point 2.

POWER POINT 2

THE FIRST LINE YOU WRITE

MUST HAVE ABSOLUTE 'BITE'

YOU MUST GET YOUR READER IN

QUICKLY OR ELSE YOUR LETTER

WILL GO STRAIGHT

TO THE WASTE PAPER BASKET.

That Power Point really says it all doesn't it?

Clearly, your reader is going to make up his mind about reading your letter quickly—very quickly.

Either the opening 'grabs' him in some way or leaves him cold.

In fact, your reader will quickly decide—**based on what he's read in your opening few lines only**— whether or not he reads on. So, whether or not your letter gets the *action you want* depends heavily on your opening.

It is clearly one of the most critical aspects of your letters. That's why you'll need to take note of. . .

POWER POINT 3

INVEST AT LEAST 80 PERCENT OF YOUR TIME

GETTING THE OPENING RIGHT

AND MAKE CERTAIN

YOU GIVE IT SOME 'BITE'

In other words, those first words you write are absolutely critical. You see, if people read the first 50 words, they'll read the next 5000. Clearly then, we want them to read those first few words. We want them to be sufficiently impressed, stimulated, aroused, curious or annoyed, *to read on*.

In other words, we want that opening to have IMPACT and draw the reader in. We want it to stimulate some reaction— either negative or positive—but some reaction nevertheless.

We certainly don't want a zero reaction or apathy.

You probably feel comfortable with the idea of impressing, stimulating and arousing your reader early. And even the idea of making them curious makes sense. But you may question the wisdom of creating a 'negative' reaction. The wisdom is this. A negative reaction is far better than a 'nothing' reaction.

To illustrate that, consider the case of a client in the Housing Industry. They were building and decorating a new Display Home. They understood **REACTION** and **IMPACT**.

So, instead of the 'normal' colour schemes they decided to do the entire interior scheme in black and white—no other colours—just black and white.

To promote the home—to get people to visit the Display Home—they used a Radio Ad with this basic theme:

> **'You must come and see the black and white Display Home. You'll either love it, or you'll hate it. But you must come'.**

Love and hate. Powerful words. The result?

People came in droves.

And when they came, they met with salespeople in the Display Home who had been trained specifically to deal with both the love and the hate reaction. For example, when a visitor would leave, the salesperson would ask,

> 'By the way, how did you like the home?'

Let's suppose the visitor said,

> 'Wonderful . . . that decor is fabulous'.

Then the salesperson would say,

> 'You know, it's certainly a high fashion look—by the way, when were you planning to build?'

Or, if the visitor said,

> 'Ugh, it was awful, couldn't stand the colour scheme'

the salesperson would respond,

> 'You know, I'm not at all surprised you feel that way. After all, it *is* very different. Tell me, what sort of decorator scheme would you prefer?'

Clearly, either extreme reaction is far better than a visitor saying, 'Oh, it's O.K. I suppose'.

Clearly too, we would all prefer the opening of our letters to have a positive reaction. If that's not possible, then you should go for a negative one…but more about that a little later.

You'll always get reaction when your openings are short and sharp. Like in this example of a complaint letter to the Telephone Company.

Good Morning,

Please notice these two words…

Good morning.

They're friendly. They're courteous. They're warm.

In fact, they're everything that Telstra isn't.

Now that's a challenging sentence isn't it? I want it to be challenging. Because this *is* a complaint letter. And because I'm a customer I hope you'll respond positively to it.

Let me explain that.

You see, in general Telstra has a bad image. Now I know you're working at changing that – and very successfully in some areas. And I've seen your excellent ads that are designed to give us a better image of Telstra.

And the new phone system you installed for me recently is excellent.

Yet the image that most people have of Telstra comes from your people. People who operate the 12 455 directory service. People who operate the 132 203 residential faults service. And the 12 454 wake up and reminder service.

Call them.

There's no courtesy. No 'good morning'. No 'thank you's' or 'pleases'.

Nothing . . .

Just an irritable sounding voice.

All it takes to change that is a concern for your customers. It doesn't take millions in advertising. Just a few thousand dollars on some Performance Standards so that your people can perform effectively and represent Telecom better.

You know MacDonalds treat their customers brilliantly. They have Performance Standards for their people. And people like to deal with them. Telecom by comparison . . . Well, you figure it out.

But I know you *want* to provide good service. I don't know of course how many transactions you handle each day. But I do know that each one is a golden opportunity to build the image. Right now, the image is being broken not built.

I'm looking forward to hearing from you.

P.S. Perhaps when we talk, we can discuss where you can get those Performance Standards I spoke of—I do know a place.

To show you more about 'reaction' in action, one of our friends was writing a mailing piece. He's an advertising man who helps people put effective ads together. He deliberately wanted to set a low key tone to the mailing piece. So it began . . .

'Would you like some help with your advertising?'

Sometimes when you're writing advertisements, you're too close to the action to write them effectively. This was one of those times for our friend. He wasn't happy with the headline (even though it is low key.) It's not very strong and there's a danger that it will have a 'ho-hum' type of response.

We discussed it and decided that a punchy headline would have far more effect.

The solution? Give it the 'punch' to make it even more effective *yet still low-key* by using what is called The Third Party Referral technique.

Here's how the final version ended up.

> 'At last. Someone has cut out all the rubbish and
> 'hype' and come up with a commonsense approach to
> advertising . . . that WORKS!'

Clearly that has more 'clout'—more impact. And it gets even more impact by using the Third Party Referral (notice the quote marks.) You see, when you use The Third Party Referral technique you use what someone else said to give your opening added strength. That opening was, in fact, exactly what one of our friend's clients had said.

So, your openings must have punch and impact.

The key? Use short, simple sentences. Even single words standing alone.

For instance, let's look again at the opening lines in this Chapter. To save you turning back, here they are again.

> This is it.

> The part of the book that will make you say 'I'm glad I
> invested in this'.

> You see, have you ever stared at a blank piece of paper
> and wished that **SOMETHING** in fact **ANYTHING**
> would come into your head? But nothing did?

> You have? Then we're on the same wavelength.

Notice the simplicity of the words—particularly the first 3. They're short. And as a direct result, they have impact.

Here's an example that illustrates the point clearly. It's a letter from the General Manager of Australian Airlines . . .

Good morning Mr Pease,

I'll make this brief. I'd like to talk plainly with you.

Our nation's getting a lot of bad news lately.
If we all sit around waiting for someone else to solve the problems, things will go from bad to worse.

So instead of talking, this airline is doing what has to be done.

We're raising the standard of our game in every way.

And we're giving it all we've got.

It won't be easy, but nothing worthwhile ever is.

This booklet will give you an idea of just some of the things we're doing.

One final thought.

I'm not a pessimist. I believe that the problems Australia is facing can and will be solved with less gloomy talk and a bit more dedication.

Our airline now bears the nation's name.

In return, we'll give the nation an airline all Australians can be proud of. You have my word on it.

You see the common thread?

Short, sharp sentences. Sentences of just a few words. Just one idea at a time. 'Paragraphs' that are really simple sentences.

Compare those examples with the opening on this letter . . .

Dear Sir,

XYZ Insurance has established a strong and respected position within the London business community by providing a professional and complete insurance service. In attaining this standard of service, XYZ Insurance has recognised that a client's insurance requirements extend beyond just a document to protect a Company's financial assets or legal liabilities.

Pressures on senior management in all business enterprises to maximise profit and reduce losses are far greater now than at any previous time. Meeting these pressures requires the support of a progressive Insurer with access to current, accurate information.

XYZ Insurance has available specialised facilities to help you. These include Loss Prevention (property and liability), Employee Safety, and Engineering.

The availability of these services, together with our flexibility, responsiveness and above all absolute security, have made XYZ Insurance a leader in the business insurance field in this country and. . .

Here, it's much harder for the reader to get involved with the letter isn't it?

It's boring. It has no impact.

It's got long paragraphs and sentences. It talks all about XYZ Insurance. There's no WII-FM.

As a direct result the reader is *not* involved.

But what we've just seen in that letter happens frequently. No wonder letters get thrown away.

But from now on you're going to be different—particularly in the openings of your letters.

From what we know so far, the keys to letter openings are:

Make it short
Make it snappy
Give it 'punch'

As well as those, the airline letter we've just seen uses another technique to rivet attention. A little phrase that literally demands that you sit up and take notice.

'I'd like to talk plainly with you'

You can use that strategy to break through the clutter too.

For instance, take a look at this letter from a top Accounting Firm. But before you look at it, put yourself in the position of one of their clients. As a client of this particular firm you're used to getting letters from them and in the past, those letters have been what we'll call the usual 'stuffy' Accountants' letters. You get your mail and you see an envelope that has on it:

HOW TO WALK THROUGH A MINEFIELD
. . . AND MAKE IT EASILY TO THE OTHER SIDE

Intrigued, you open the letter.

Good morning Stephen,

I'd like to talk plainly with you.

Put very simply, computer systems can be a total pain in the butt.

You've probably heard the stories. We've seen them in real life. Potentially brilliant computer systems creating disaster areas in business.

> *Not only that, any business thinking about getting involved with computers these days is faced with so many choices. Unfortunately though, choosing becomes like walking through a minefield.*

It's dangerous. That's the bad news.

There is, however, some good news—very good news.

First, when you're correctly advised, it's now possible to get really great computer performance for your business at far less than $15,000. Secondly, and perhaps most importantly, you can profit from our experience. We've found a way to guide you safely and inexpensively through that potential minefield.

> *In fact Stephen I'd like to invite you to take just one hour out of your day sometime in September. In return, I'll donate one hour of my group's time to you. It's completely free—no strings attached.*

During that hour you'll discover a way to meet your business needs—a way that will be unique for you.

You'll get plain talking from us—no sales promises, no 'hype'. You'll get advice that will make sound business and economic sense. In short, Stephen, it's an hour that'll save you heartache, time and money. I personally guarantee that.

> *And, we'll be able to let you in on some surprising information on some new business computer products—information that could mean a great deal to your business.*

As I said, there is a way out of the computer minefield I'd like to share that with you soon. I'm certain that you can begin to profit from our experience.

There are two ways to take advantage of this special offer. Simply call me on XXXXXX or complete and mail the coupon I've attached for you. We'll then set a time when you can come in.

You'll appreciate that the available consulting hours will be filled very quickly Stephen so I do urge you to respond as soon as you possibly can.

I'm looking forward to hearing from you.

P.S. If for some reason I'm not available when you call, ask to speak to Peter Smith or Jennifer Barnes. They're fully qualified to help you through that minefield too.

You'll notice several important things here.

First, the letter really does talk 'plainly'. Or, to put that another way, it tells it like it really is. You see, we could have said,

> 'There are so many computer systems around today,
> it's difficult to know which one to choose'.

While that's true, it doesn't paint the right picture. And the right picture is that choosing the wrong computer can lead to disaster.

So you need to paint that picture.

And you do that by using powerful analogies. Like the minefield for instance. Analogies create powerful pictures in your reader's mind.

You will have also noticed something else about the opening of that letter.

The so-called 'salutation' or greeting. Let's look at it in more depth.

Tradition has it that your letters should begin with 'Dear John' 'Dear Sir' 'Dear Mrs Smith' or worse still, 'Dear Sir/Madam'.

Let me let you in on a secret (that's yet another excellent opening phrase, by the way.) When writing letters, *never* use 'Dear' anything.

Why?

Well can you imagine meeting the recipient of your letter face-to-face and saying 'Dear John' or 'Dear 'Sir/Madam'? You wouldn't do it would you?

You'd say 'Good morning John' 'Hi Sue' 'Hello Mr Smith'. So why don't we do exactly that in letters?

Tradition. Conformity. And that's why every letter that comes out of our office begins . . .

'Good morning John'
'Good morning Mrs Stevens'

or simply,

'Good morning'

You'll recognise that last phrase is extremely useful, particularly if you're using a Word Processor to produce 'standard' letters to a Mailing List.

Let's explain that.

You might have a list of people to write to. You may have the christian names of some of those people on the list. But some might be on your list as 'The Manager'.

When you merge* your standard letter with the mailing list you put a merge symbol after the opening. Like this: 'Good morning *', then in cases where the list contains the name, your Word Processor will look up the record and come up with 'Good morning John'.

But where the name isn't on the mailing list, you simply leave a blank in the appropriate record and your word processor letter begins . . .

'Good morning'

It's so much better and so much more effective than 'Dear Sir' isn't it?

And there's another valuable reason for using 'Good morning' 'Good afternoon', 'Good evening' 'Hi' or 'Hello' as a salutation.

*Merging refers to taking a standard letter with what are known as 'merge codes' in it. This standard letter is then merged with a mailing list and each merge code is automatically replaced with appropriate data on the list.

It immediately stamps your letter as . . . different. Right up front. And that's more than worthwhile. Just that alone improves your chances of your letter being read.

And on top of that, it can easily lead you into a superb opening. Like this for example . . .

Good evening Tom,

You'll notice I'm writing this at night.

There's a very special reason for that Tom. You see, I wanted to take time right now to thank you for a great meeting earlier on today.

You see, in the short time we were able to spend together, you gave me a very clear insight into what you're striving to achieve within XYZ Company. And that helped me get exactly the right perspective on how our Bank can help. I appreciate that very much.

Now that kind of opening leads us nicely to another way of opening your letters so they hit the mark right away. It's called the 'Compliment Opening'.

Before we work at developing it, let's take a step back to discuss compliments in general.

You know, the simple act of complimenting other people is becoming a forgotten art. We just don't seem to do it that much anymore.

Yet, in not doing it, there's no doubt at all that we're missing out on a tremendous opportunity—an opportunity to build people. Specifically, an opportunity to build up your reader.

Perhaps you feel that compliments are 'gushy'. Flattery is gushy. Genuine, sincere compliments, expressed correctly are superb relationship builders.

Here's a good example of how a Compliment Opening leads your reader into your letter.

Hi Bob,

It really was a delight having you over here on Tuesday. Thank you so much for making the trip and for contributing to an enjoyable morning.

Your ideas on a 'launch' of our programme to your Service Advisors in early August sounds great and I'm looking forward to getting your initial letter on that. As well, I'm looking forward to working with your people.

But . . . that's not the purpose of this letter.

Our purpose is to look in more depth at those training videos you brought over with you. You saw my reaction Bob. They are very, very good.

And here's another one to someone who's perhaps a little more business-like.

Good morning Mike,

It is good to talk with you Mike—we seem to be able to sort through the 'fuzz' and get to the key issues.

> *It's rare to see that in business these days. So . . .*
> *thank you for your excellent contribution.*

Going back to our discussions last Tuesday and to your letter (the 11th August one), you'll recall you asked me to get back to you with some additional details on how we propose to go about solving what you call **'THE IMMEDIATE PRIORITY'**. . .

Take time to get used to writing 'Compliment Openings'. They'll work wonders for you. You'll see more examples as you continue reading. (And you might want to note that the technique of paying sincere compliments is covered extensively in Allan Pease's book, TALK LANGUAGE.)

Here's another idea for you on openings. This one may shock you. Imagine receiving a letter that opens this way:

Good morning Bill,

I goofed.

What would you do?

You'd read on, right? We've grabbed your attention and you'll read on.

Just to prove the point, here's the beginning of a very creative letter that uses the 'I goofed' concept. Notice how it makes you want to read on.

15th January

Good morning Jane,

I missed a deadline. Or to put it bluntly—I goofed!

This letter is 15 days late. It should have been dated 1st January.

That's because I made my New Year's Resolution exactly five months ago to the day. *And you're about to find out what it was and why it's so important to you.*

But first, let me explain what's been going on late at night for the past 22 weeks . . .

You see, you really can be creative and hence different. When you are creative your letters will start being effective.

Here's another 'shock' opening that worked wonders. We wrote it for a photographer who wanted to write to prospects in the Public Relations business. He felt they had a need for his service.

As you'll recognise, our photographer was prepared to be different. Not only did he mail the letter, he included an excellent (and free!) mini-print of a magnificent red MG car with each letter. Here's the letter opening.

Good morning John,

By the time you finish reading this letter you'll want to do one of two things:

    *   *pick up your 'phone and ring me*
or *   *throw this letter in your waste paper basket*

Now at this point you've just got to read on to figure out which option you'll take. And, just in case you would pick the latter option, the photographer has you covered . . . read on.

But . . .if you take that last option, you'll certainly want to keep the free mini-print I've sent you (and you'll see that has my 'phone number on it too!) Some people would call that 'gotcha'.

Now at this point, your smile will broaden. As a result, you'll read on again. And then the letter gets right in on WII-FM.

Well—I hope I have. Because this letter may well help you get even better results (bottom line results) for the clients you serve. And I guess that just has to help you.
Let me explain.

You see, some people think I'm crazy. That's because people tell me I've got a unique ability to capture creative thoughts on photographic film. People like Grant Noble, the Australian Sales Manager of National Computer. He said:

'. . . your photographs were, without any question,
the telling difference between success and failure of
our product launch. Truly brilliant stuff . . .'
And exactly that kind of difference John, can now be yours . . .

It's good. It's different. That opening is a 'classic' And above all, it works.

Yet another way of being different and making sure your letters get read is to use the Quotation or Third Party Referral technique opening. This is where you refer, directly or indirectly, to a third person (or group of people) to make the point.

You've already seen one example of this earlier on—the example about our friend in advertising. Here's another one to illustrate the point.

Good morning,

Image!

People say it's a critical aspect of companies who continue to succeed.

And they're right.

Your corporate image is enhanced (or reduced) by the style and quality of your communication with customers and suppliers. Not only that, in the purchasing function especially, you know only too well how critical it is to save costs, and avoid wastage so . . .is it possible to do both, create a brilliant image and save money at the same time?

That's the purpose of this letter.

You see, we have a way through new IBM technology *of helping you to do both brilliantly.*

So that you can see just how effective these new typewriter products are, I will be calling you within the next week to set a time when we can get together. Not, I might add, to talk about how great these new products are, but first to discuss your specific needs.

You'll be receiving my call soon. Until then, please continue to enjoy. . .

. . . great things.

. . . .

P.S. Nearly forgot! Thank you for taking time to read this. I'm certainly looking forward to meeting with you.

Notice here the one word opening followed by the quote followed by an indirect compliment ('They're right.')

Here's another example—this time in a Direct Mail piece mailed to Accountants to get them to come to a seminar.

Good morning,

I'd like you to study this quote very carefully . . .
*   'Seven years ago, I thought Accounting was just*
*   about being a good Accountant. Then the light*
*   dawned. As a direct result we've gone from 2*
*   partners to 8—from 1 office to 4. And on top of that,*
*   revenues have increased 6 times".*

The speaker? Now one of Australia's best known Professional Accountants.

You see 7 years ago, that man listened to two of the most exciting speakers in the world on Professional Marketing— Paul Dunn and Allan Pease. Now, by an exclusive arrangement, you can invest just $95 to hear Paul and Allan speak in Singapore. And we literally guarantee that you'll get a brilliant return on your investment in the evening.

Let me explain . . .

On Tuesday 16th September, by being at our Seminar with Paul and Allan, you'll discover exactly how to build that all-important marketing edge into your professional practise. You'll immediately see powerful ideas that really will work for you.

You see . . .

So that's the Quotation Opening. Soon we'll look at how we build from the opening. But first, one more classic opening technique. This one is called 'Promise-A-Benefit-in-the-Opening-Line'.

Clearly, to use this effectively you need to thoroughly understand the WII-FM concept in Chapter 2. And you also need to have a good grasp of human motivation. This next Power Point gives you that grasp.

POWER POINT 4

PEOPLE ARE MOTIVATED TO

1. MAKE A GAIN

or,

2. AVOID A PAIN

In other words, people will do things (or buy things) to gain something they don't have or to avoid the loss of something they already have.

Period.

So, to promise a benefit in your opening line, you need to hone in on a possible GAIN or possible LOSS. Whether you pick GAIN or LOSS will obviously depend on the type of person you're writing to.

For example, let's suppose you're marketing a new office copier and you're directing your letter to the Marketing Manager or Sales Manager of your target company. Naturally, marketing or sales people are going to be more turned on with GAINS.

So your letter might go like this:

Good morning Mr Hannon,

This may come as something of a surprise.

You see, it's now possible for you to dramatically increase the amount of business XYZ company gets from quotations and proposals.

Let me explain.

New developments in high-tech copier technology mean that
you can . . .

Now let's suppose you're marketing the *same product* to the *same company*. But this time, you're directing your letter to the Finance Manager. The Finance Manager is much more likely to be turned on by AVOIDS. So your letter might begin this way:

Good morning Ms Rees,

You probably see copiers as a necessary evil.

They can certainly eat up costs can't they? So . . . this may
well come as something of a surprise.

You see, it's now possible, using proven developments, to
totally avoid wastage of corporate funds.

Let me explain.

See how it works? And notice how we use 'gain' words (as in 'new' and 'increase') to the Marketing Manager and no-risk words (as in 'proven') to the Finance Manager.

But what if you're not sure which approach to take? Then use both, like this. . .

I'd like to talk plainly with you about 3 key things in your
business.
        Your Sales . . . increasing them
        Your Image . . . improving it
        Your Costs . . . reducing them

You see, it's now possible for you to achieve those increases
and those savings in your business with new yet already
proven technology.

Let me explain . . .

So far we've looked at openings as they relate mainly to what might be called sales letters. And it's true that *any* letter you write to *anybody* is, in fact, a sales letter.

After all, your purpose is to 'sell' an appointment, to 'sell' a product, to 'sell' an idea, to 'sell' an on-going relationship or to 'sell' someone on doing something you'd like them to do.

Whatever you're writing about, you're always selling something. It's important to recognise that. Because when you understand this your letters will get noticed, get read *and* get acted upon.

Like letters that you might send to collect money from debtors. When you think about it, those letters really are 'selling'. They're trying to 'sell' the reader on taking a certain course of action they've not taken up until now.

You need to 'sell' them on responding immediately. Now you could choose to do that with threats. Or you could learn to do it much more effectively by using the ideas in this book. In fact, you'll see Chapter 9 is devoted entirely to effective money-collecting letters.

You'll find too that these ideas can be used in your personal life. Like in this example of a *very* personal letter.

Good evening Jodie,

This is a late night letter.

It's now 2 in the morning. My bedside light is glowing softly. And I'm thinking of a very special person.

You.

Since we met briefly yesterday, I've seen your face a thousand times. You absolutely captivated me.

Sure . . . I wanted to say that yesterday but there were too many other people there and . . . I didn't want to appear 'forward'.

But sometimes a guy has to pluck up courage to do certain things. This is such a time.

Let me explain that.

You see Jodie, I would like to see you again—to get to know you better—to spend some time with you.

So I'll be calling you soon to do that so that we can arrange to go out on, say, Saturday?—perhaps to a great little restaurant I know you'll like.

Until then, enjoy

. . . good things

P.S. I'll call you at work if that's O.K. If it isn't, just call me on 8372109.

Already you've seen that letter openings are crucial. And now you see it's quite easy (by using these skills) to construct openings that get read.

Sure, it takes practice. But it's a major key to writing letters that work.

So . . . you've used your openings to literally grab your reader's attention.

You've used simple words. Short, sharp sentences. You've said things like, 'I'd like to talk plainly with you'.

You've used compliments—maybe Third Party Referrals.

You've given your opening some punch, some impact. And as a result, you've grabbed your reader's attention.

What's next? How do you hold that attention? How do you get to the point? Let's find out . . .

Four

How to Get to the Point

Already you understand thinking 'outside the box'. You've grasped WII-FM. And you've grabbed the reader's attention with our opening. What now?

Here you're into the body of the letter. Well, not quite.

First you need to 'link' from your opening. You need to establish a kind of 'flow' from the opening.

Let me explain that.

You see, you need to change step, to set a new tone of giving your reader the key information that *he needs* to lead him to the decision you'd like him to make.

And right there you've seen 'linking' in action. The key phrase 'let me explain' followed by a new paragraph beginning with 'You see . . .' achieved the correct change of pace.

'Let me explain' effectively says to your reader . . .

> 'O.K. I've given you my opening approach. I've grabbed your attention. Now, settle back and open your mind. Make it ready to accept new information that will carry you along a rewarding path'.

And the 'you see' opens the gate to the path.

Read on through these examples so that you can follow (and then use) the techniques.

This first example might be an interesting one to use when you want to get a raise.

Good morning Boss,

'Oh no!'

That's how some bosses react when they're asked for a raise.

If you did react that way, then the purpose of this letter is to see if we can move the 'oh no!' to at least a 'maybe' and the 'maybe' to a 'certainty'.

Let me explain that.

You see, you and I know salary increases aren't always motivators - they don't necessarily encourage people to work harder.

Salary increases like this one are best when they are a reward for effort already put in.

You already know of the effort put in to lift our productivity. And, it's really good to have those pats on the back that you give.

In the past 12 months though, my salary has remained static. Yet productivity and effectiveness have increased.

I understand that salary increases are difficult. Just how much should they be, for instance?

That's probably best sorted out when we meet to discuss the ideas. I'll have some facts and figures with me then so that you can make the appropriate assessment.

Working with ABC Company is good and I'm looking forward to many more happy years contributing to its growth.

I'm looking forward to discussing the salary increase with you.

Gillian Thomas

P.S. Perhaps we could make it Wednesday this week?

Here's another example—this time a letter to a Council about their building regulations.

The Town Clerk
City Council
City Hall
Paddington.

Good morning,

Effectiveness.

You're correctly concerned with it—in particular the effectiveness of the use of land.

That's why this letter is important.

You see, this letter is specifically to request **the relaxation or variation of certain building regulations** *so that a more effective use of the dwelling and land at* **187 Willowood Road, Paddington** *can be established.*

Let me explain.

We currently operate a Word Processing Bureau service from home (it's the subject of a separate letter to you).

You understand that operating a business from home does have its advantages—one is that it's hard to 'switch off'—to get away from work so to speak.

With that in mind we've tried to find solutions which are:

   (a) economical so that the business can continue to grow

   (b) structurally sound

   (c) environmentally 'additive'—that is—solutions which create a more effective use of space and the environment

We believe we've found that solution and understand that to adopt it will require a variation to certain building regulations.

As you'll see from the plan attached our land fronts Fernberg Road. However, the plan does not really show the true situation.

Let me explain.

Part of Willowood Road has, in fact, been blocked off. . . . . . .

And here's another example of linking in action. This time it's a difficult situation—telling a lover 'goodbye'.

Tony,

Music, they say, is the food of love.

And sometime in the future, you and I will hear a tune. We'll both get a lump in the throat. We'll maybe even cry.

Because it will remind us of the good times we've shared. The times that now must come to an end.

Let me explain that.

You see, the spark that once was there, is no longer. And I need that spark to burn.

And you do too Tony. But now I need my own space again.

Yet although there's no spark, we will be friends. In a while I'll call you to see how well your life is going.

But don't call—the hurt would be too much right now.

Knowing you has been . . .

. . . beautiful.

And one final example—this one a 'lead-generating' letter that might be used by a salesperson who sells Financial Services. The letter is to preface a phone call from the salesperson to set up an appointment with his prospect.

Good morning,

Remember yo-yo's?

They go up and down, up and down.
    Just like our savings sometimes. It's as if you have
    holes in your pocket. You try to save and then the
    money just seems to disappear. And you're back to
    rock bottom again.

It's one of those bad habits isn't it? But now there is a way to kick it. Permanently.

Let me explain. . . .

You see, it's now possible for you to iron out those bumps. And for as little as just $10 each week invested in you and your future. In fact, that $10 can quite easily turn into a six figure sum over a surprisingly small period of time.

You'll be getting a call from me soon so that we can arrange a time to get together so I can show you exactly how it's done. I think you'll be impressed.

Until then . . .

P.S. When we meet, I'll show you exactly how to make certain your financial yo-yo stays up!

Now in some letters, the link from opening to 'body' can be done differently. Particularly in sales with letters you write following a visit with an existing or potential customer.

In letters like this, you move from opening to 'body' by **ESTABLISHING YOUR PURPOSE** and by **BACKTRACKING**.

Let me explain (there it is again!)

Consider this scenario (that's another 'linking phrase' for you).

Let's say Allan has been called in by a company to talk with them about training their staff.

He's used the meeting *not* to talk about how good his training is but to *uncover their real needs* . . . or to put that another way, to find out where they're at, where they want to be, what they want the training to achieve and so on. He's ended the meeting by going through a few quick ideas and by promising to get back to them in writing *so that decisions can be made.*

The opening of this letter presents an ideal opportunity to compliment. And an ideal opportunity to get the purpose right.

Take a look. You'll see it's almost self-explanatory.

Keith Moine
ABC Life Company
P O Box 1022
AUCKLAND N.Z.

Good morning Keith,

You probably get a lot of letters that begin by saying something like this:

> *'It really was good to meet you on . . .'*

Well, this is another one.

Because it certainly was a delight to meet you on Friday, Keith. We had not just a pleasant and enjoyable meeting but a purposeful one as well.

> *You were able to outline exactly what you wanted to achieve in your 4th November Conference. You gave me an insight into what ABC Life is all about and that certainly helps in putting together a programme for you.*

You'll recall I promised to get back to you with some ideas. That's the purpose here Keith—to give you those ideas so that you can be even more in tune with the contribution we'll be making to your group (and so that you see you'll be getting excellent value for your investment.)

Just to check that we're on track, let me quickly review what you told me:

* **You want to cultivate a 'customer-centred' attitude within the office.** *As you said, anybody who calls ABC Life is either an existing or potential customer. They have to be dealt with in a way that's consistent with that. And, as you pointed out, your prime customers are your agents. You want to make sure that when they deal with ABC Life, it is a pleasant experience. After all, those agents could well go elsewhere.*
* **you want to build an 'esprit-de-corps'.** *It's important to cultivate an environment in which people feel motivated—one where they can excel—one that has that certain 'feeling' about it. Achieving that automatically lifts performance.*
* **you want to build up skills.** *From what you said Keith, many of your people who deal with customers have not been trained to do that effectively—they perhaps lack 'finesse' in certain areas.*
* **you're well aware that the telephone is your 'shop window'.** *How clients are greeted and treated on that piece of plastic and wire sets the tone for the entire organisation. Perhaps there needs to have a set of standards developed—perhaps a set of standards that lay down the key customer-focussed behaviours you want to achieve.*

Putting all that together does suggest a fun, exciting and very valuable three and a half hour programme Keith.

Let me explain . . .

The key phrases that do the linking from opening to 'body' and establish your purpose are these:

> *You'll recall I promised to get back to you with some ideas. That's the purpose here Keith—to give you those ideas so that you can be even more in tune with the contribution we'll be making to your group (and so that you see you'll be getting excellent value for your investment.)*

> *Just to check that we're on track, let me quickly review what you told me:*

And then we let the reader do his own selling in effect by telling him what he told us. Reviewing like this establishes a 'nod factor' with the reader—he nods in agreement as he reads your letters because, after all, you're telling him (perhaps in more emotive language) what he told you. So it's the most natural thing for him to nod in agreement.

Here's another example so that you can see how effective 'linking' can be for you:

Donald English
56 Anywhere Street
Anytown.

Good morning Donald,

It was good to talk to you by phone on Wednesday.

Although we were fairly rushed, we were able to get into some important details about your needs. So . . . thank you for taking the time to do that.

Just to make sure we're on track, let's quickly review what we're trying to achieve:
* *you want to achieve a pool setting that completely blends in with your surroundings*
* *you want to create an environment which is totally relaxing on week-ends*
* *you feel it's important to have an area where your children can play safely*
* *you want areas of cool shade to get away from the hot sun and,*

* *you want decks where you can comfortably suntan*

I've given some considerable thought to your ideas Donald.

Let me explain. . .

Here we've used key 'bullet' points to highlight the key areas. In fact, the prospect in this case didn't tell us these things exactly this way . . . but he would have if he could have expressed it this way.

You'll see much more on this key idea in Chapter 8 which deals with Quotations. But from what we've covered already you should see the point. Linking, backtracking and establishing a purpose lets your letters 'build' naturally.

You move from your powerful, impactful opening to the body of your letter by opening the reader's mind.

You do that with phrases like:

Let me explain
Consider this scenario
Picture this scene

or by moving from the opening by clearly stating your purpose. Tell your reader '. . . our purpose here is to do (such and such) so that you will achieve the desireable result.'

And, if you've previously met your reader, link to the body of your letter by reviewing what he told you during the meeting.

Linking like this keeps the reader's attention in high gear.

Now let's see . . .

Five

How to Effectively Build the Letter 'Body'

Picture this scene.

You arrive at your favourite restaurant with your favourite person accompanying you.

The Maitre d' welcomes you—escorts you to your favourite table and offers you a free aperitif.

You enjoy the 'small talk' as you're drinking your aperitif. And then the Maitre d' comes over again . . .

'Ze chef, 'e 'as prepared, 'ow you say, 'is specialty of ze 'ouse for you. Eet is not on ze menu but I know you weel enjoy eet—eet is sensational. Weel you accept my recommendations . . . yes?

And you accept.

Ten minutes later, the Maitre d' appears carrying 'ze specialty of ze 'ouse' on a large silver platter covered with an equally large silver lid.

He places the platter on your table, lifts the lid and says 'May I weesh you . . . bon appetit'.

At this moment, you look down at the platter and see. . .

TWO BIG, RAW, PEELED ONIONS

Nothing else. Just onions.

So, somewhat annoyed (since raw onions aren't exactly your favourite food) you get up and leave the restaurant.

Disappointed. Annoyed. Vowing never to return again.

And that's exactly what can happen with letters too. Your readers in effect get unpalatable non-exciting things (like onions) and they mentally 'walk away' from your letters.

But back in the restaurant our Maitre d' has learnt the error of his ways.

His next customer for 'ze specialty of ze 'ouse' gets onions too . . . but this time they're a little different.

Picture this. There's a bed of rice attractively laid out. On the rice is a skewer. And on the skewer is a little piece of onion, followed by some capsicum, followed by a magnificently cooked cube of meat or seafood. And that's followed by another piece of onion, another piece of capsicum and another succulent piece of meat or seafood . . . and so on.

The food is hot, the aroma enticing. Your taste buds can hardly wait.

Notice the different? That unpalatable onion has been turned into something you want to eat.

You'll discover how to add that capsicum and succulent meat to your onions right now. You're going to discover exactly how to make the body of your letters 'edible' so that your reader is 'hungry' to read your words.
To do that, let's look at a letter we've already seen.

Dear Sir,

If your Company is in the business of giving advice about computer related solutions for importing, warehousing and distribution, merchandising or manufacturing—please read on.

Our Company is planning a series of Presentations at the Sheraton Hotel on 3rd and 4th September. Attendance is by invitation only, and is designed specifically for persons who regularly advise their clients in such matters. The Presentations are the same on each day, in order that you can choose which day is convenient for you.

If you wish to attend, please call Robyn Donovan on (. . . . . .), so we can send you a formal invitation.

Yours faithfully,

. . . .

What's in it for me? Nothing. There's no WII-FM.

Well, maybe there is but the letter certainly doesn't tell me about it, does it? It's full of unpalatable onions.

So, remembering WII-FM and onions, let's see if we can re-write the letter to make it palatable (and to pack people into the Seminar).

Good morning Mr White,

You've got a difficult task to carry out.

After all, advising clients in a professional way *about computing is not easy.*

That's why this letter could be very important to you.

> *You see, by coming to our special Consultant's Seminar on 27th September you'll be able to make your job a little easier. And you'll be able to do an even better job for your clients.*

Let me explain . . .

You see, when you come to the Seminar, you'll be seeing for yourself some new exciting ideas and techniques never before seen in Australia. Techniques that I'm certain will excite you.

For example, you'll see some completely new 'networking' systems in action. What this means to you is you'll be able to connect systems together in a new way. So that they work more effectively. And so your clients' existing systems become more productive.

But more than that. . .. . .

You see, it's a matter of talking in the reader's language isn't it? We all know we should do that, but we frequently end up with onions.

For example, let's suppose you received a letter from a friend about this book. In the body of the letter your friend could say something like this . . .

> '. . . in the book there are lots of examples of letters for every occasion'.

But that's an onion. And the phrase '. . . there are' is impersonal (it's better to say 'you'll discover'.)

Now it's absolutely true (as you know) that there are lots of example letters here. Yet just saying it—just expressing the fact on its own does nothing for the reader.

So, let's change it around. Here goes!

'You'd naturally expect your book to be full of example or sample letters. In fact, you'll find 58 of them—each one full of new and powerful techniques for you to use.

But more important than that is the way each letter is clearly set out so that you can relate easily to the ideas. As you read them, you'll almost certainly find yourself underlining key phrases—phrases that make each letter literally 'come alive' in the reader's mind.

Perhaps most importantly of all though, you'll discover exactly how to put these letters into action in your business and personal life. Almost immediately.

It means that your letters will have that added 'something' to make them and you memorable to the reader. No more staring at blank pages. And no more letters that make you (and your reader) cringe. And above all, you'll see and be able to write letters that get acted upon positively'.

O.K. It took more words to say it. Just like it took a few more ingredients to make our onion more palatable in the restaurant.

But it *didn't* take much more *effort*. All it took was a little time for you to think about your reader. And then it took a few key phrases—phrases that *automatically* have you 'talking' in the reader's language.

We'll identify those phrases for you in a while. But first let's touch on something that might be important to you.

And that's this. You may feel that it isn't necessary to take things as far as we're suggesting. You may feel that the reader understands exactly what it means to him to have sample letters in a book on letter writing.

Truth is . . . you're absolutely right! The reader does (in many cases) understand what's in it for him. The BIG PROBLEM is, he may UNDERSTAND THE NEGATIVE.

Let me explain . . .

Suppose I said to you . . .

'the book has lots of sample letters in it'

You could think . . .

'Hmm, I bet these are all letters that the author has written in his style about his business. I bet they won't relate to me'.

Or even . . .

'I don't have time to go wading through hundreds of letters—I'll give it a miss'.

You see, you may assume the negative.

Your readers could do that too if all you give them is onions. Starting from now, promise yourself *you'll never again take the risk of letting your reader think the negative.*

Or, to put that positively, promise yourself that you'll make your reader see a positive picture. Make life easy for your reader by always telling him what's in it for him.

The question is, exactly how do you do it?

One of the best ways is to stop occasionally as you write the letter and say to yourself . . . 'so what?'

Or, perhaps better still, as you're writing, picture yourself talking face-to-face with your reader. And hear him interrupting occasionally with this question, 'How do you mean?'

Phrases like 'so what?' and 'how do you mean?' will force you to expand on your onions in the reader's terms.

Next we use Link Phrases to make the onions taste good.

Let's look first at Primary Link Phrases so that you can see how they work, in simple terms.

These are two of them:

SO THAT YOU . . .

and

WHAT THIS MEANS TO YOU IS. . .

Here's how those phrases work for you.

FACT	LINK	WII-FM
The book has lots of sample letters in it	**SO THAT YOU**	can see exactly how easy it is for you to apply the ideas in your business and personal life
OR		
This book has lots of sample letters in it	**WHAT THAT MEANS TO YOU IS**	you'll be able to see precisely how you can use the ideas immediately in your business and personal life

You'll recognise how we've started to talk in our reader's language by using the Primary Link Phrases. And those phrases force you to write like that easily.

Now we can really ram home the message by using the Final Link Phrases so that we stress the GAIN or PAIN factors we spoke about earlier.

The Final Link Phrases are:

MOST IMPORTANTLY. . .
NOT ONLY THAT. . .
THE REAL BENEFIT TO YOU IS. . .
MORE THAN THAT. . .

Here's how they work to build **POWER** into your letters.

> **AND, PERHAPS MOST IMPORTANTLY** your letters will start to really work for you, building business and getting the results you want.
> OR
>
> **AND, NOT ONLY THAT** you'll see that your letters are really getting read at long last, not thrown in the bin, making the effort it took you to write that letter *worthwhile*.
> OR
> **AND, THE REAL BENEFIT TO YOU IS** you'll be able to adapt the ideas to your own 'style' so that the real meaning and the real 'you' comes through loud and clear.
> OR
> **AND MORE THAN THAT** you'll see how your readers will be able to get *in touch* with your letters, relating to your ideas the way *you wanted* to relate to them. No more staring at blank pages. No more wasted time. Instead—letters that work.

They are powerful phrases aren't they? And simple to use.

Once you get used to using them you'll find that it becomes normal to write (or talk) this way. And you'll find other groups of words too that help you relate easily to your reader.
Take a look at this next example—a letter written to Building Contractors. As you read it, I suspect that you'll start picturing yourself owning and actually using the product that's the subject of the letter. You see, using these link words will put your reader in the picture too—the picture *you* want to create.

Good morning,

You know, trying to make an honest dollar today can be pretty damn frustrating.
> *You want to make more money. But to do that sometimes costs more than you've got. I think it's called Murphy's Law.*

For example, you want to employ a secretary let's say. Someone to take messages for you. Someone who can call Mrs Jones and tell her you're on your way. Someone who can help do what you do best.

But . . . that's going to cost you an arm and a leg—about $1800 per month in total.

Well, there's now a brilliant new solution. One that can dramatically boost your business very quickly.

It's called . . . **GIRL FRIDAY**

Let me explain what it means to you and how it works.

It means a **dramatic business boost.** *One of our subscribers can show you figures which show we've helped him boost his business by a staggering 69 per cent in less than twelve months.*

It means no more lost phone calls *that could have resulted in profitable business for you. And, most importantly, it means no more driving around looking for a phone to call people back. And it means* no more lost business *because people didn't talk to your answering machine.*

How's it work? You'll find that it is remarkably simple. Here's what happens. . .
> *We equip your vehicle with a smart looking telephone handset. You're out on a job somewhere and your office phone rings . . .*

Your GIRL FRIDAY answers it. Promptly. Professionally. Depending on your instructions she'll take a message or, in some cases, act on the message immediately.

Then your handset in your vehicle buzzes. You're told instantly of the message **AND HERE'S THE EXCITING PART**.

You can then talk directly to your GIRL FRIDAY and ask her to deal directly with the caller or pass on a message. There and then. (As one of our clients said, try doing that with an answering service or try doing it with a pager! You can't!)

And it sure leaves an answering machine for dead!

You see, GIRL FRIDAY gives you lots more. More than a message service. In fact, it really is like having your own personal secretary without paying for one.

Whatever you call it, I know just how valuable this brand new service is.

But that's not really important.

What is important is that you have the chance to see it for yourself.
So, here's a really sensible idea.
1. As soon as you've read this, pick up your phone and call Rosemary or Trevor on XXXXXX
2. Tell us you'd like to know more and we'll arrange for you to see the service in action in your business without any obligation.

As we said, it is now possible to have a pleasant and extremely helpful lady in your office (without having a lady in your office) when you need it most.

I'm looking forward to hearing from you.

Sincerely,

P.S. When you call, remind me to tell you more about the businessman who boosted business by 69%. It's an incredible story. It could be your story too.

You'll notice that this letter breaks one of the *supposed* 'rules' of good communication—keep it short.

The reality is you want to get your reader *involved*. You want to keep that 'pace' going—to keep that sizzle. And the more involved your readers are, the more likely they are to take the action you want them to take.

So, with one exception, let's replace that old 'rule'—keep it short—with this Power Point:

POWER POINT 5

THE MORE YOU GET YOUR

READER INVOLVED

THE MORE LIKELY THEY ARE

TO TAKE THE POSITIVE ACTION

YOU WANT

But, you need to be very careful. You see there is one classic exception to that new Power Point. And that's when you're in sales and writing what might be called a 'lead' letter.

As we've seen before in Chapter 4, a Lead letter is a business letter where your sole purpose is to preface a 'phone call to make an appointment with your prospective customer.

Clearly here you must only tell your reader a little. After all, if you told them *everything*, there's absolutely no point in them seeing you. Here's an example you've seen before that does the job very effectively:

Good morning,

Image!

People say it's a critical aspect of companies who continue to succeed.

And they're right.

Your corporate image is enhanced (or reduced) by the style and quality of your communication with customers and suppliers. Not only that, in the purchasing function especially, you know only too well how critical it is to save costs, and avoid wastage so . . .is it possible to do both, create a brilliant image and save at the same time?

That's the purpose of this letter.

Let me explain.

You see, we have a way through new IBM technology *of helping you to do both brilliantly.*

So that you can see just how effective these new typewriter products are, I will be calling you within the next week to set a time when we can get together. Not, I might add, to talk about how great these new products are, but first to discuss your specific needs.

You'll be receiving my call soon. Until then, please continue to enjoy. . .

. . .great things.

. . . .

P.S. Nearly forgot! Thank you for taking time to read this. I'm certainly looking forward to meeting with you.

So with that exception, remember

THE MORE YOU GET YOUR READER INVOLVED THE MORE LIKELY THEY ARE TO TAKE THE POSITIVE ACTION YOU WANT

When you use these ideas you'll find that your letters 'bristle with sizzle'. You'll write each sentence with real 'sell'—keeping your reader's attention.

So, let's review where we've been so far.

You must think **outside the box** and get into **WII-FM** thinking mode.

Your **openings** are a real key—they must have **impact** and **punch**.

Then you link into the body by opening your reader's mind— phrases like **consider this scenario** or **let me explain**.

And in this Chapter we've seen exactly how to build the body of your letter.

We've seen how onions are unpalatable. You must use **Link Phrases** to make your ideas 'come alive' in your reader's mind.

And what that means to you is your letters will get read. Not only that, your ideas will be understood *positively* by your reader.

No longer will your letters be dull and boring. Sure, they'll be longer. Yet your reader will enjoy what he's reading. He'll almost see you in the room talking with him. And that's great writing.

But, since you'll most likely be writing longer letters now, you'll need to use some neat little techniques to keep your reader involved. And you'll discover exactly what they are in the next Chapter—it's called . . .

Chapter 6

How to Keep Your Reader Reading— Involvement Techniques

So far, we've looked at key concepts and words to help you *and* your reader. Here we'll look more at the techniques of laying out your letters so that you keep your reader reading.

And after all, you want to do that. Because soon you're going to ask him to take some action—the action *you want* him to take.

Here's one such involvement technique. The indented paragraph.

> By indenting a few key paragraphs you do 2 things. You highlight that paragraph *and* you break up the letter so that you dramatically *improve* the readability. Makes sense, doesn't it?

So, a letter that would have looked like this . . .

Mr Peter Smith
Manager—Communication Systems
Scope Systems
1 Nichols Road
Perth WA 6000.

Good morning Peter,

Friday in Melbourne was good. Thank you for the prime part you played in making it that way.

Thank you too for outlining the opportunity we have to improve the work flow and effectiveness in your organisation—in Head Office initially. In that sense, the lunch you organised with other management personnel was profitable too in that it helped clarify some of the key issues.

Certainly, some things need more time for clarification but one thing is crystal clear—that Mission Statement, ' . . . achieving high profitability by satisfying customers' needs . . .' is absolutely the centre of our focus. It's also crystal clear from your Research that, in Head Office at least, the current telephone approach makes it difficult to carry out that mission.

You'll recall, Peter, that I promised to get back to you with an initial framework which will help us to see a clear path to implementing a system that succeeds. And that's my purpose here.

It's worth highlighting that what your surveys reveal is most likely only the tip of the iceberg. As Rex observed, with your business expanding rapidly, it's going to be increasingly difficult to rectify problems without major disruption.

Let me explain that. . .

With indentation it now looks like this . . .

Mr Peter Smith
Manager—Communication Systems
Scope Systems
1 Nichols Road
Perth WA 6000.

Good morning Peter,

Friday in Melbourne was good.

Thank you for the prime part you played in making it that way.

> *Thank you too for outlining the opportunity we have to improve the work flow and effectiveness in your organisation—in Head Office initially.*

In that sense, the lunch you organised with other management personnel was profitable too in that it helped clarify some of the key issues.

Certainly, some things need more time for clarification but one thing is crystal clear—that Mission Statement, ' . . . achieving high profitability by satisfying customers' needs . . .' is absolutely the centre of our focus.

It's also crystal clear from your Research that, in Head Office at least, the current telephone approach makes it difficult to carry out that mission.

> *You'll recall, Peter, that I promised to get back to you with an initial framework which will help us to see a clear path to implementing a system that succeeds. And that's my purpose here.*

It's worth highlighting that what your surveys reveal is most likely only the tip of the iceberg. As Rex observed, with your business expanding rapidly, it's going to be increasingly difficult to rectify problems without major disruption.

Let me explain that. . .

Clearly, it's easier to read and as a direct result *it will be read!*

So, use indentation to keep your reader involved—to make it easier for them to read your thoughts.

Another involvement technique is *the 'feedback question'*. You saw it a couple of paragraphs ago, didn't you? Just 'popping in' the odd rhetorical feedback question (but don't overdo it) emphasises the one-to-one communication you're having with your readers. And it keeps them involved by getting a 'nod' every so often.

Doesn't it?

In fact, questions can create a great deal of reader involvement in your letters. That's particularly true with Complaint letters.

Here's an example of the use of the technique in a complaint letter written to the Postal Authorities in Australia. So that the opening phrase in the letter makes sense to you, it's important for you to understand that the Australian Post Office has a slogan, 'We Deliver'. Here's the letter in full.

The Manager
Customer Service
Australia Post

Good morning,

We deliver!

It's an excellent slogan and I'm certain your mail delivery statistics are good.

The question is—are you delivering *service* to your customers?

> Based on our experience over 9 months now dealing with your Cityville Branch Office, the answer is 'no'.

We've made at least 2 'phone calls to complain but now it's time to put it in writing.

Let me explain.

From your customer's stand point, the office is a real disaster.

Walk in there like a customer does. You'll notice something immediately (aside from the queues.) There are no smiles. It's seen that the customer is regarded as an interruption to the staff's day—and not the reason for their existence.

MacDonalds would have gone broke years ago if they allowed this to happen.

> Things are done at snail's pace. And to make matters worse, you might stand in line for 11 minutes (as I did this morning) whilst people who walk in later get served in another line.

And what's more, interruptions that counter staff get from their colleagues are handled with much more courtesy and speed than we customers.

But it doesn't stop there. Private Box mail is very rarely sorted totally by 9.00, 7.30 was once the norm. We could put up with this if we were treated pleasantly as human beings when we go to the Post Office.

Is it the staff's problem? Or is it Management?

Well, that's for you to sort out I guess. I wish you luck in trying to get it heading towards anything approaching satisfactory.

If this is 'Excellence' in action, I guess I've read a different version of the book.

In our office we have a sign on the wall. It says this:

Customers Are Really Everything (you'll see it spells **CARE**).

That might be an important motto for you to adopt.

We can't deal with anyone else but Australia Post.

All we can do is tell you what's happening in the knowledge (or hope) that someone cares enough to do something about it.

Let's hope something . . .

. . . happens

P.S. I sincerely believe you do care otherwise I wouldn't be writing this letter to you.

As well as showing the effective use of a question, this letter also shows some of the techniques we'll be talking about later in the book. What it doesn't show is Australia Post's response.

Their response was magnificent. Within 24 hours of the letter being sent, we had a phone call from the Customer Relations Manager of Australia Post. Within 3 days we had a visit to discuss the situation. And within a week, the staff at the Post Office concerned had been 'moved sideways'. It goes to show how effectively written letters can get the response you want.

And it shows how you can get your reader involved with your letter.

Let's look at some more involvement strategies.

An interesting one is the use of double "rabbits ears" or single 'quotes' like that.

They literally BREAK UP sentences (just like brackets and CAPITALS do as well) to make the sentences *even more readable*. And you'll notice that <u>underlines</u> can be used as well . . . but not too many at a time. O.K?

As we've said, when you apply the ideas in this book the likelihood is that you'll be writing longer letters (but you'll be composing them better *and* quicker than ever before). So you must work at keeping your reader's involvement right through your letter.

Here's a great little technique that will do that for you. You'll see it at the bottom of the first page of this next letter.

Good morning,

By the time you finish reading this letter you'll want to do one of two things:
*   *   pick up your 'phone and ring me*
or   *   throw this letter in your waste paper basket

But . . .if you take that last option, you'll certainly want to keep the free mini-print I've sent you (and you'll see that has my 'phone number on it too!) Some people would call that 'gotcha'.

> *Well—I hope I have. Because this letter may well help you get even better results (dollar and cents results) for the clients you serve. And I guess that just has to help you.*

Let me explain.

You see, some people think I'm crazy. That's because people tell me I've got a unique ability to capture creative thoughts on photographic film. People like Grant Noble, the Australian Sales Manager of National Computer. He said:

> *'. . .your photographs were, without any question, the total difference between success and failure of our product launch. Truly brilliant stuff . . .'*

And exactly that kind of difference . . .(name), can now be yours.

Imagine. No longer the 'standard' stuff that produces a kind of

. . ./2

Now isn't that interesting? You turned the page.

Once again, you've seen how applying the traditional 'rules' actually work against you. You see, you've been taught to end pages at the end of paragraphs.

But by NOT DOING THAT, in fact, by creatively breaking your page right in the middle of a key idea, you literally force the reader to turn the page and get much more involved. Make sense?

And the more involved they are with your letter, the more likely they are to take the action you want them to take.

So . . . keep your reader involved by using involvement techniques like:

>   CAPITALS (but please use them sparingly)
>
>   <u>underlines</u>
>
>   **bold type**
>
>   heavily indented paragraphs
>
>   "quotation marks like this"
>
>   or 'like this'
>
>   and asking questions

Critical . . . aren't they?
So now, you've learnt:

* to think outside the box

* that your reader is tuned in to the special WII-FM station

* to open your letters creatively

* to 'talk' in WII-FM terms—to turn 'onions' into edible morsels with Link Phrases

* to use involvement techniques to keep your reader's attention

Let's now find out . . .

Seven

How To Get the Action You Want—Closing Your Letters

Ever seen a letter that ends like this?

> *'Assuring you of our best attention at all times?'*

Yuk!

It says nothing. Well, it's perceived by your reader that way. So why say it?

It's formal. We'd never say it like that in real life. It's a cliche. And it's overworked.

In a while, you'll discover some new ways to finish your letters. Right now though, let's review where we've been.

Actually, I'm kidding—we're *not* going to review where we've been at all. I simply wanted to suggest a review because . . . it's a great way to start the closing part of your letter. Simply review the key points. Like this:

> *Also Mike, you see here the value of a staged and structured approach to the training. Here, new material keeps coming at your people rather than the 'old' way of giving them the whole lot and hoping they do something with it.*

So, let's just review what we've said.
*   * you'll have a programme that keeps building with fresh ideas each month to keep your people involved and eager.*
*   * your people will be getting and absorbing material that's totally relevant to them—it means they'll be using each skill immediately. And as importantly, you'll see the results just as quickly.*

These are just the initial ideas Mike. As I said, the purpose is to use them as a framework.

You'll need to digest the ideas and see how closely they match with your views. And how closely they relate to the real needs.

Looking at our current work schedule, we could start into the programme towards the end of September. Again, I'm not certain how that kind of timing fits in with you. Clearly, we need to take a look now at the options and get together so that the ideas materialise into action.

I'll be calling you soon Mike so that we can arrange to do that. Until then, my thanks again for such a pleasant initial meeting.

Keep at it and keep on enjoying good things

So what you've done as you've built up the letter is the classic TELL TELL TELL—that is you *tell* the reader what to expect (in your Opening and Purpose) you then *tell* them what it is in WII-FM terms (in your Body) and then you *tell* them what you told them in your closing section.

But, since your letters now have PURPOSE, you must leave your reader knowing exactly what action to take or what action you'll be taking to follow up your letter.

And that leads us to this key concept:

IF YOUR LETTER IS NOT ASKING FOR AN ORDER (as in a Direct Mail piece, for example) MAKE SURE YOU'RE IN CONTROL OF THE FOLLOW UP.

Now the person who wrote this next letter didn't understand that.

Dear Sir/Madam,

RE: STAFF DEVELOPMENT AND TRAINING PROGRAMS

Further to our recent telephone communication with your company, we have pleasure in enclosing our brochure for your perusal.

As your Company is aware, training and development of personnel plays a vital role in the success of a company's operation. The enclosed information highlights the courses available which could be suitable to your needs by providing an alternative training to your existing programs.

Please call for an appointment to inspect our in-house training facilities, or we can arrange to call and see you should you wish to obtain further information on course content and availability.

Your faithfully

Who's in control here? Whose court is the ball in?

Clearly in this case, the reader is in control. It's up to him whether or not he gets back to the company. Surprisingly this letter was sent *after* the reader had responded to an ad. Amazing. . .but true.

In other words, the reader had already indicated to the company that he was interested.

Yet this letter effectively dulls that interest.

Clearly, when they call asking for information on your products or services they're telling you that they are in the marketplace— they're telling you they want to buy.

Responding to that type of call with a letter like the one you've just seen switches off that interest.

It ends by putting the reader in control of any follow-up.

Now you might say '. . . but the company could still ring the reader because they said they might.'

Well that's true, they could. But then the reader may well perceive it as 'pushy'. So please don't end your letters like this:

'Please feel free to call us, or we'll call you if we haven't heard from you.'

That close is O.K. in an accounts letter asking for payment but not elsewhere.

So, the close on that letter could have been more effectively handled this way:

Again, it was good to hear from you Miss Truscott. Thank you for taking the time to get in touch.

You'll be receiving a call from me within the next few days so that we can check that we've responded correctly to your needs. And we may be able to confirm a trial enrolment for you in one of our upcoming programmes.

Until we talk, do continue to enjoy . . .
        . . . . many good things

P.S. By the way, I've checked course availability for you ahead of time. We do have a vacancy on the 11th March Programme (that's about 16 days away) so you might like to check that out in your diary before my call. Thanks in advance for that.

You see, in this case, there's no doubt about who is in control, is there?

Yet it's expressed in a helpful way ('.. you'll be receiving my call *so that . . .*')

It's not 'pushy' - well, it's giving a little nudge that's true. But why not? After all, in this case the reader called the company to get a brochure. And that alone is a great expression of interest—what in selling terms is called a 'Buying Signal'.

She didn't just call the company because she wanted a brochure. As we said, she wanted to buy—not necessarily from that company, not necessarily their product and not necessarily today.

But clearly by ringing for a brochure, she is in the marketplace. So that new method of closing the letter edges the reader a little closer to buying, doesn't it?

So, as we said, make sure (whenever possible) that **you're in control of the follow up**. Like in the potentially delicate matter of asking a neighbour to pay for half of the cost of a fence as in this next example.

Good morning Joan,

It's not often that you get a letter like this—one that's from one door away from yours.

So . . . since a letter from your next door neighbour is rare, then it must be about something very important.

It is.

You see Joan, over the years that we've known one another, we've both done things to build up the value of our properties.

> *And maybe you've thought (as I have) that putting in a modern fence between our properties would help improve both our values. And that's true.*

And that's why it's standard practice for neighbours like you and me to share in the investment in a fence.

Right now Joan, I'm not sure what type of fence would look best. I'd appreciate some feedback from you about what your preferences are.

Meanwhile Joan I've received some information on budgets and styles. You'll see I've enclosed some details for you on that.

I'll drop by soon so that we can discuss prices and styles and select the right fence for both of us. Until then . . .

P.S. I'm looking forward to hearing your views.

Here's how that same idea of keeping control might be expressed in a sales letter inviting a potential customer to a launch of your new product—in this case a new range of desks.

Good morning Peter,

Yawn and
yawn and
yawn.

Maybe that's happened to you when you've gone to new product launches. You know the kind of thing—people ask you how it was and the nicest thing you can say is 'The food was good'.

Well, here's a product launch that's different!

*You see, by coming along to a special function on 11th November you'll be amongst the first to see and take advantage of a brand new office furniture system that recognises this truly **is** the start of the 21st century.*

It's a furniture system that recognises we have telephones, that recognises we have computers, that recognises we have FAX machines. In fact, it's so good it's just been awarded an International patent.

We'll be calling you to make sure you don't miss the launch Peter. And I'm certainly looking forward to seeing your reaction . . . I think you'll be more than impressed.

Until we meet, continue to enjoy . . .

. . . good things

P.S. To make it even more exciting, we're giving away a special door prize too. So, why not call now on 229.6754 just to let us know you'll be along?

Sometimes, there are situations where you can't be in control of the outcome. Take, for example, a Direct Mail piece mailed to say 2 or 3 thousand people.

In these situations however you can actively encourage your reader to take action.

You do that by using THE OFFER TECHNIQUE.

Direct mail and advertising specialists will tell you about the power of AN OFFER. Using an offer is a strategy which encourages response.

In fact, there's a manual on advertising called 'The Do It Yourself Guide To Small Business Advertising' which shows the results of a $1,000,000 study. The study proved that an offer that is perceived as valuable to the reader will boost response by as much as 300 per cent.

Take a look at how Paul uses the offer technique in the last few paragraphs of the letter he mails about the Outgoing Telephone Call programme.

Phone Right Part 2 has so much in it that: a) it's a full 4 hour programme and, b) it's taken me quite a few words to tell you just a little bit about it.
So . . .maybe you deserve a reward for reading this far and for acting on what you've read. Let me explain that to you now.

> *Although Part 2 is an eight part, four hour programme, your investment in it is $198 and that includes the Part 2 Pocket Guide which contains excellent reinforcement material. And I guarantee that you'll get much much more than that back in increased business.*

However, when you order your copy by completing and returning the Order Form, for an extra $11 only, we'll automatically include Part 3 of the programme for you provided your order is sent prior to 29th August.

Part 3 is normally a $98 investment so by ordering Part 2 and Part 3 now you'll save $87 right away and have two great programmes working for you.

Part 3 is that part of the programme that your secretary and/or receptionist will love because it shows her some excellent new ways to do her job even more effectively.

She'll automatically enjoy her job even more too and become a more effective member of your team. (Some users tell me that the first part of the programme is really great for anyone *who might be needing a performance lift.)*

> *But don't just take my word for it. Just complete the Order Form now for Part 2 at $198, decide to add in Part 3 and try both. If you find,* for whatever reason, *that you don't benefit from them, simply return them within 21 days for a full and immediate refund.*

Once again, it is delightful to have you using and benefiting from Phone Right. I'm looking forward to hearing from you soon.

Until then, continue to enjoy . . .

. . . many good things.

You'll note that the offer, to be effective and believable, must have a time deadline. And it even works after the closing date.

Recently Allan had a 'phone call from someone who'd picked up a magazine with an ad in it. The magazine was 22 months old!! And yet the caller began by saying 'I've just noticed your ad. Is that offer still available?'

Such is the power of offers.

There's another closing strategy has a lot of power too. It's the humble 'P.S.'

The 'P.S.' is very important. For example, on a single page letter you often go straight to the bottom of the letter to see who it's from. While you're there, you just happen to notice the 'P.S.'

Or on a lengthy letter, say 3 or 4 pages, the 'P.S.' will be the last thing read so it gives you the opportunity to convey an important message in a way that really makes it stand out.
The 'P.S.' is like the asterisk in an ad headline. When we see the asterisk in the headline we tend to read quickly through the ad to find out what the asterisk refers too, don't we? It gives the ad extra impact. Just like a 'P.S.' on a letter.

Here's a good example of the 'P.S.' used in a letter applying for a job:

Good morning Mr Stewart,

Today your mail is big.

You've probably received many letters applying for the job you advertised in Saturday's Newspaper—the job for a sales assistant.

Well, it's my plan to make this letter stand out. You see, my purpose here is:

   * to let you know something about me
so that
   * we will be able to arrange an appointment
so that
   * I will be able to start contributing to the goals Angus Hardware is achieving

Let me explain.

Good salespeople need to be enthusiastic. I am. It means you'll be getting someone who gives 100 percent effort.

Good salespeople (or any employee) need a positive outlook on life. I have. You'll see my smile rubbing off onto others.

And my sales skills paying off in results.

And good salespeople must be honest. I am. So you can rely on your customers being treated with care. (You'll see more about that in the references and job history I've enclosed for you.)

When I work with you Mr Stewart, you'll discover my philosophy is that 'you get back what you give'. With that philosophy of 'contribution' in mind, I'm looking forward to meeting you and to working with you.

Sincerely,

P.S. I am keen to meet you and start with you so I'll be calling you on Tuesday so that we can arrange to meet.

The 'P.S.' drives home an important message.

In this case the message is that the writer is 'different'.

And a letter like that will help him get the job.
So, adding in a 'P.S.' is important. In fact you can add even more impact by handwriting the 'P.S.' (providing your handwriting is legible). It adds a real personal touch. And it adds power.

The 'P.S.' is so important (studies show it can increase response to your letters by up to 25%*) that you may well want to deliberately omit a key point in the body of your letter just to keep it for the 'P.S.'

Or, just use it to re-emphasise a key point in a different way like this letter sent to attendees at one of Paul's seminars:

*That reminds me. Numbers expressed numerically like this '25' have much more impact than numbers expressed this way 'twenty-five'. So break the 'rules'. With the exception of the beginning of sentences always write numbers *not* words. And don't express them like this 'payment terms are net seven (7) days' - it's unnecessary and goes back to the dark ages. Just 7 is fine.

Good morning,

Speakers speak.

And audiences listen.

> *But last month when I had the privilege of speaking
> with you and your colleagues at The Gateway, you
> did much more than listen.*

You gave me something special. A gift.

Let me explain that.

*During our conference you gave me so much in terms of
involvement, and positive feedback. I felt part of the team.* I'll
always remember that.

*Sure, we shared some ideas to help you achieve. But now I'm
able to offer you something even more powerful.*

> *You see, on Wednesday, 11th June I'm bringing my
> friend Dr Denis Waitley to Brisbane. And I want
> you to share in the special evening Denis has
> planned.*

*You'll probably know of Denis from his books like 'The
Psychology of Winning', 'The Double Win' and 'The Seeds of
Greatness'. His work is recognised throughout the world—by
U.S. Astronauts, by the U.S. Olympic team* and*, very
importantly, by your company. You'll see more about that
when you go through the brochure and Registration Form
enclosed for you.*

Go through it now. And decide to be with us on 11th June.

*Thank you for all you gave me. I'm looking forward to seeing
you on 11th June. Until then, continue to enjoy . . .*

. . . many good things

PAUL DUNN.

P.S. There's something special for me to mention that you won't see on your brochure. Simply this. Denis' new material is such tremendous value you might want to consider bringing along someone in your family between 14-18 years. It'll help them and you enormously. And to make that possible, I've reserved 100 seats for your family members at very special rates. When you call to register for the Seminar, be sure to ask for more information about this.

Now that last 'P.S.' is nice isn't it? It adds power, believability and warmth.

In addition to the 'P.S.' you'll notice we're not ending off letters 'Yours faithfully', 'Yours sincerely' and so on.

Just like you'd never greet anyone face-to-face by saying, 'Dear Bill' so you'd never leave them by saying 'Yours faithfully'.

Again, the reason we do it is tradition. And doing it makes your letters send like everyone else's—dull.

Instead of these hackneyed phrases, use the close of your letter to *be different* to re-emphasise effectively the difference that is you.

(In fact this 'difference that is you' is so important, later in the book you'll see a Chapter dealing with The Difference That Is You. You'll find it useful as a very effective summary of all we're getting across in this book.)

Closing your letters with phrases like:

> *Enjoy. . .*
> *. . . good things*

is like beginning them with 'Good morning'. It keeps that relaxed conversational tone you've established in your letter and stands out as different.

And it gives you an easy way of 'wrapping it up' like this:

> *Again John, It was good to meet with you. I'm looking forward*
> *to working with you and, to talking with you soon by 'phone.*
> *Until then, continue to enjoy . . .*
> *. . . many good things.*

The phrase 'until then' provides a tidy link to the ending. Here are some more examples:

> *'Until then, do make sure you keep on enjoying . . .*
> *. . . increased sales.*
> *'Until we meet on the 15th, be sure to keep . . ..*
> *. . . at it.'*
> *'Again Julie, I appreciated getting your note, let's be sure to*
> *keep staying close.'*
> *'You'll be receiving your programme next Friday John, and*
> *I know you'll enjoy and benefit from it. If anything comes*
> *up in the meantime, do be sure to keep . . .*
> *. . . in touch.'*
> *'It's good to be working together with you Bill, I'll be doing*
> *my utmost to make sure your sales . . .*
> *. . . soar.'*

Phrases like these will sound strange to write, so much so that you'll be inclined to resist changing them.

But be aware that there are 2 critical impressions people get— the first impression *and* the impression you leave them with.

So, how you close your letters is almost as critical as how you open them.

And the key ideas on closing are:

> * *review the key ideas of your letter*
> * *make sure you're in control of the follow up wherever*
>   *possible*
> * *use an offer to stimulate positive and immediate*
>   *response*
> * *use a P.S. and handwrite it to give it even greater*
>   *power*

and then,
> * *compliment the reader or wish them well—much*
>   *like you would in the face-to-face situation*

We're delighted you've read and enjoyed the book so far. We'll make certain you continue to discover . . . many more ideas.

Like those in the next Chapter.

Eight

How To Get Results from Tenders, Proposals and Quotations

Someone once said, 'If I had just $1 for every quotation that ends up in the waste paper basket, I'd be rich.'

And it's true. Many quotations do end up in the rubbish. And many quotations end up not achieving what they set out to do—which is just as bad.

Why is that?

Because so many quotations are laid out the wrong way. And they all look the same. Some achieve results—*but few achieve the result you want*. Even fewer convey the feelings you want to convey.

In fact, most quotations are nothing more than a list of services, products and prices. Not only that, they invariably give the reader or potential client more reasons NOT TO BUY than reasons to buy.

And you may have noticed how most quotations force the potential client to focus on the wrong things. Like price for example. Most quotations actually force the user to consider only one thing—PRICE. They invariably force him to compare your price with someone else's—they force him to get other quotes.

So (unfortunately for you) price becomes the key issue in the quotation or proposal. In fact, that's *all* most quotations focus on. And to make matters even worse, the price is usually featured strongly AND, most important of all, it's usually the last thing the reader sees.

It's even underlined in red sometimes to make it stand out even more!

And what's that conveying?

Simply this. That the reader should base his decision on price. AND THAT'S NOT WHAT YOU WANT TO CONVEY. IT'S A RECIPE FOR DISASTER.

Let's illustrate the point.

Take this quote for something simple like window cleaning.

BETTER WINDOW CLEANING
Quote Number 00307
Mr Peter Allen
187 Fernberg Road
Paddington Qld 4064.

To:
Clean Windows at above
premises on a monthly basis: $ 130 per month
Total Price for year: $1560

TERMS STRICTLY NET SEVEN DAYS

And contrast it with this:

Good morning Mr Allen

It was good to meet the you on Wednesday.

Thank you for taking the time to show me through your property. It certainly is an impressive location and your home, with so much glass in it, really lets you take advantage of the views. Provided, as you said, that your windows are kept beautifully clean.

> *From what you told me, it seems like your idea of arranging for them to be cleaned on a monthly basis would be best. And that means that you can take advantage of yearly rates. From what we discussed your monthly investment will be just $130. And that includes a number of key services.*

Let me explain. . .

You'll be receiving a professional and thorough service using only new high-tech window cleaning fluid. These new products are guaranteed by us to leave absolutely no film or residue.

And that of course means that your windows stay looking cleaner much longer. As well as that Mr Allen, your French Doors (all 8 of them) will require and get special attention, particularly in those small hard-to-get-at corners, so they continue to look as good as new.

> *And, perhaps most importantly of all, you'll be able to take advantage of a unique, no-quibble performance guarantee. If ever, and for whatever reason, you find that the work is not carried out to your total satisfaction, you'll be able to simply call me direct and arrange for it to be corrected.*

With our experience with homes like yours however, it's very unlikely that will occur. But I guess it's nice for you to know that a guarantee applies.

Again Mr. Allen, it was good to meet with you. I'm certainly looking forward to having you as a valued and long term client.

With best regards,

. . . .

P.S. As we discussed, we'll be in touch on Monday so that we can confirm all the details and perhaps start the initial cleaning on Wednesday 15th.

Now clearly (no pun intended) there are a few comments to be made about this.

First, this is just an example to illustrate the point. Any window cleaning company worth their salt would employ professional salespeople who would be able to confirm the order on the spot during the visit to inspect the job so that a quotation or proposal would not be necessary.

Secondly, it takes a little extra time to do a proposal like this— about 5 minutes I guess. But is it worth it?

I think you'll agree that the first quote will only get the business if it's the lowest price. The second version has a far greater chance of *selling* for you. And so it has a far greater chance of getting the business REGARDLESS OF PRICE DIFFERENCE (within reasonable limits).

So, what are the keys to writing quotations or proposals like the second one?

Perhaps the most important one is:

GET THE PRICE OUT OF THE WAY EARLY

The reasons are:

* Putting price at the end forces the reader to give price primary consideration
* Putting price early lets the reader consider all the benefits of dealing with you as *the last thing* he sees
* It's a 'no-surprise' way of doing it. Many times, people give their products a great big build up early in the letter and then let the reader down at the end with the price.

Once you GET THE PRICE OUT OF THE WAY EARLY it then gives you ample 'room' to expand on your product and service features. But not just features (or 'ONIONS') but real WII-FM benefits.

Doing it like this leaves the reader considering the *value*, not the price. And that's absolutely vital.

Now that window cleaning letter was a simple example, but it did illustrate the point.

Here's one that's a little more complex. As you'll see it certainly highlights the principle of GET THE PRICE OUT EARLY.

Good morning Mrs O'Callaghan,

It's been good talking with you and Mr O'Callaghan over the past weeks. Your ideas on design and quality are very much in line with ours.

Because of that, we're really looking forward to working closely with you as we build your new home. It's going to be a home that we'll all be very proud of.

You'll recall you asked me to confirm our discussions to this point so that we can go ahead and put the appropriate wheels in motion. That's the purpose of this letter Mrs. O'Callaghan – to let you know of your investment in your new home and what that entails.

Let's look at that investment area first.

From what we've discussed your investment will be $287,840.00 and that is based on the enclosed plan we've drawn up specifically for you.

You'll see we've taken care to include the following things that are important to you.

1. *Your rear fernery will be constructed much like a pergola with pavers to the floor, a fence to the rear and a gate to the side for easy access. And, importantly, you'll keep out those annoying insects because we'll be fully enclosing the area with shade cloth.*
2. *Your front verandah will have that same shade cloth treatment and it will have pavers on the floor. That means it will make it even more enjoyable and prestigious.*
3. *We'll be including for you a remote controlled garage door to make life a little easier when it's raining.*
4. *Your driveway will be* paved *right from the boundary to the garage door. This will add significantly to the perceived value of your home, particularly for re-sale so it's a wise investment.*
5. *All of your kitchen* and vanity tops will be tiled and have a timber edge strip to add further to the good looks of the home.*
6. *You pointed out the need to have two drawers for clothes baskets, Mrs O'Callaghan. We'll be including that for you together with two ceiling fans.*
7. *Your bathrooms will look great with the addition of a spa bath, a Jacuzzi pump and air switch. We've included these items for you. In addition to these areas it's worthwhile detailing just some of the things you'll be getting* automatically and without additional charge *as an Easybuild Homes client.*

You'll see some separate sheets attached for your reference file. They give you specific detailed figures to make sure you're fully informed and to protect you from any price escalation.

Again, the entire team at Easybuild Homes are looking forward to working with you both. We're looking forward to a long and pleasant relationship.

Sincerely,

P.S. I nearly forgot! You'll see I've enclosed the formal acceptance form for you. You need simply to approve this document by putting your signatures in the places I've indicated and return it together with your initial $500 deposit to allow detailed plan drawing to get underway.

It's a great proposal isn't it? It puts all of the ideas we've seen so far into action.

You'll notice too how it gives the reader many reasons to do business with the Company concerned. And you'll notice how it cements the relationships that have been established in the face-to-face meetings.

Certainly, the examples we've seen so far are relatively simple. Sometimes you may be involved in negotiations that are more complex.

But even in the more complex cases, the ideas you're learning in **WRITE LANGUAGE** can be applied. Certainly, in some cases you may need to be a little more formal. When those situations arise, we recommend that you set out your proposal with separate sections covering the following key areas *in this order*.

* A room where food is prepared. People can't resist asterisks can they?

Purpose

Use this brief section to cover the major objective of the proposal—what the people you're writing to will achieve (in broad terms) when they accept your proposal.

Background

Remember that other people (other than those you've spoken with) will be reading your proposal. So use this 'Background' section to talk briefly about who you've had meetings with in the organisation. As well, highlight the key points that came from those discussions.

The Needs

This is one of the more critical areas of your proposal. Use it to tell them what they told you. This section is really where the selling is done—it shows you've listened and that you're on track with what the organisation wants to achieve. Ideally you should bring out here not just factual areas but emotional ones as well.

The Investment

Many organisations submit proposals with pages and pages on how good their product or service is and then they have a section at the end of their proposal called 'Cost Justification'. PLEASE DON'T DO THAT for the reasons we've already outlined.

Instead, deal with the pricing (or investment) in this special section right after 'The Needs'. And when you get it out early, give the total figure first and then break it down as appropriate.

Fitting The Needs—Achieving the Purpose

This section heading may well change depending on your product or service.

Here you describe your product and/or service AND YOU DO THAT IN WII-FM TERMS. In other words you tell the reader *what* your product and service is, importantly how it meets the needs and *how* the reader will benefit from acquiring it.

The Implementation Schedule

This is the last section of your proposal—importantly the last thing your reader will read. This is where you leave him with the *actions* he (and you) should now take so that all the benefits you've mentioned can start to flow.

Now there's a word in that last paragraph that is important. That word is 'action'.

The entire purpose of you submitting a proposal is to make your prospective customer take **action** on it. So—if you want to stress that fact, why submit 'proposals' at all? Why not call them 'Action Plans'.

You see, the very words 'proposal' or 'quotation' are non-committal and invite comparison. Action Plan is much more positive and says so much more.

So, that's Action Plans (or proposals)—a specialised form of a business letter. In the next Chapter you'll see another specialised letter—the one that 'demands' money.

Over the page is a different 'Action Plan' letter. It's a reference recommending a man for the position of Flight Attendant with an International Airline.

TO ROBERT'S NEXT EMPLOYER

Headaches! Headaches! Headaches!

That's what you must get in trying to evaluate suitable candidates for Flight Attendants. I'm sure most of them sound great, and present themselves very well. Which makes your task of picking the eagles from the turkeys even harder.

I travelled over 200,000 kilometres again this year, much of it with your airline. Your best Flight Attendants seem to have three things in common.

Let me explain that . . .

1. *They have the ability to communicate effectively with the passengers*

2. *They are even-tempered and polite—this means they can handle people and problems.*

3. *They are well-travelled and have the ability to carry out intelligent conversations with passengers.*

Robert Hutchinson has these three qualities. He is a "people person" who can communicate effectively with his clients, customers and friends.

He works brilliantly in a team. And he makes an excellent employee. As a bonus he is a non-smoker and a good cook! To you this means he can also converse on food and wine. Plus he is a trustworthy and a reliable worker who takes pride in his accomplishments.

I have known Robert for 12 years and have hired him in several capacities from home designer to a television actor. So, as you can see, he's versatile.

He would be a real asset to International Airlines.

And you'd have one less headache.

Allan Pease

P.S. If you would like to talk with me direct call me on 918 2486

Nine

How to Deal with Debtors—Letters to Collect Money

Anybody who tells you that new ideas will work 100% of the time has got rocks in his head!

So . . . we're not about to do that.

The ideas you'll get in this Chapter, however, will help you get money from people who owe it to you quicker than ever before. The ideas won't work every time . . . but they will increase your *rate* of success.

Here's the first idea . . .

GET THE MONEY UP FRONT

Now I know that might not be possible in some businesses but it's amazing how many can use the idea once they break down the barriers (barriers like 'that could never work here').

Of course, plumbers in particular have shown us how to do that for years. They know that the value of any service *declines* after delivery.

To explain it further, think about a situation that happened to Allan one weekend. (Unfortunately, emergencies seem always happen on weekends when penalty rates apply.) This was one of those weekends—Allan had a burst underground pipe.

He called the Emergency Plumbing Service and was told that the minimum charge would be $120 plus $35 for the use of a special machine and that charge would cover him for 3 hours.

The plumber arrived and fixed the problem in about an hour. But *before he started* he said (in a nice way) 'We'll need to fix this by cash or cheque now.'

Allan was happy to give him the money BEFORE he started just to get the job done. So . . . asking for money up front is a good idea. Let's look at how it might be done in a letter.

Keith Moine
ABC Life & Casualty
P O Box 433
Cape Town.

Good morning Keith,

It was good to hear from you in your letter of 9th September .

And it's good to know we'll be working together to achieve some key things with ABC in Cape Town.

> *So that we can keep the volume of paperwork down to a minimum (and keep on top of things at this busy time in the year) you'll see I've enclosed your invoice for you Keith.*

The normal procedure is to send 50 percent of your investment one month prior to delivery with the remainder being due on the actual day of installation.

Assuming that arrangement is O.K. Keith, let me thank you in advance for passing the invoice quickly through your Accounting Department. That'll give us both the feeling of being on top (if not ahead) of our paperwork.

I've already noticed better handling on the ABC telephones so the demonstration equipment is already working. I'm looking forward to adding to that on 6th November. Until then, continue to enjoy . . .

. . . good things

P.S. As you'll see Keith, the handsets I promised you are enclosed.

Now that letter had several key phrases which become very important when you're sending out an invoice.

The phrases are . . .

'Thank you in advance'

and,

'So that we can keep the volume of our paperwork down . . .'

Here's how they work together . . .

Jack Spratt
State Manager
The ABC Company.
GPO Box 000
Perth WA 6000.

Good morning Jack,

It really was good to be able to take some time with you in Fremantle.

Thank you for scheduling in your time and for helping so much with the installation of the computer system.

> *You know, when you go into organisations as frequently as I do you pick up a certain 'feel' about the place. Your operation has the right feel and much of that is obviously coming from you. So . . . keep at it.*

You'll see I've enclosed your invoice for you and as we discussed, I've split the hardware and software components. Thank you in advance Jack for passing the invoice quickly through your Accounting people. Doing that certainly does help keep the paperwork pile down.

Again, it really was a delight to meet you and to contribute to your progress. I'll be in touch soon to check on the results you're getting. Keep on enjoying . . .
. . . good things

Now I've checked with people after they've paid their invoices as a result of letters like this and they *really do* pass them on quicker, with more urgency, to the Accounting Department.

Now you might say that it's hard for you to do this. You might feel as though you couldn't write a letter with every invoice you send out.

Well maybe that's true.

But . . . you can include a little pre-printed note or rubber stamp on your invoices with a statement that says. . .

> Thank you, in advance, for fixing this quickly.
> It really does help us both reduce the
> paperwork pile. We appreciate your help with
> that.

So . . . there are two workable ideas for you. Let's look at a third. But first let's pose a question:

> How do you write to someone who owes you
> money for a short time—that is, when they've
> gone just a little outside your trading terms?

Just use all the ideas we've gone through so far. That is, you think in WII-FM terms, you construct a great opening that grabs attention, you give the letter some 'body' and you end it off with a neat 'close'. And, then you add a P.S.

When you do this, your letter may look something like this:

Good morning Susan,

You know, Bank Managers and Accountants can be such pains in the butt!

They do though have one very important function—they remind me occasionally that **I'm running them out of business by competing with them.**

> *'Look here Zane' they say, 'we're the ones who lend money NOT you. And you don't charge any interest either'.*

You see Susan, I've effectively loaned you $1200, the $1200 you've owed us since 5th May.

Now you might feel a little uncomfortable about that so acting on this letter may well help you feel a little better.

> *All you have to do is pop your cheque for $1200 in the mail. I'd really appreciate it if you could do that right now or please call me so that we can find a solution to the problem.*

Thanks in advance for taking some action Susan and for doing it quickly. That way we can both keep our paperwork piles down. Keep at it.

ZANE HAMILTON.

P.S. And I guess we can make at least one Bank Manager happy too!

Or maybe your money-collecting letter might come out this way:

Good morning Michael,

You know, I've tried 47 different ways of starting this letter to you. And then, it finally hit me.

All I had to do was, say **H E L P!**

All I had to do was to explain that I had a problem and needed your help. I figured you'd want to know exactly how you can help.

You see, someone in your organisation currently has an account they're 'sitting on' for $2900. Sure, it's not taking up any space but it can be annoying to have paperwork piling up.
So, you can reduce that pile and help 3 people at the same time.

First up, you'll help me. Secondly my Bank Manager will change his scowl into a smile. And most importantly, you'll help yourself by getting rid of something that might just sit there like a thorn in the side.

Thank you in advance Michael for taking action on it now. I really do appreciate your help. Keep at it and keep on enjoying

. . . good things

P.S. If for some reason you can't act NOW, I understand. But please do call me so that we can find a good solution.

Letters like this work exceptionally well in the majority of cases. And they're a lot better (and much more likely to produce good results) than the 'pay up or else' style of letter that we're so used to seeing.

As we said, it's true to say they don't work all the time but they work in the majority of cases.

And think about this too.

If you send statements to your account customers, put this book down right now.

And then go to your Accounting Department and look at a typical statement. It's almost a safe bet that somewhere on that statement will be a line like this:

90 DAYS   60 DAYS   30 DAYS   CURRENT

If you're serious about not creating a cash flow problem, then putting that on statements is, in a word, stupid.

Think it through.

What are you (inadvertently) saying? You're telling the reader that you expect them to pay in 90 days! You're saying '90 days is O.K.'

While you may want that 90-60-30 breakdown for *internal* control procedures, there's absolutely no need to tell your client. So, get rid of that line now.

Try the ideas we've gone through here. You, *and the people who owe you money* will enjoy them. And they will help bring the result you want.

And when people do eventually send you money, send *them* something important. We'll discover what that is in our next Chapter.

Ten

How To Build Relationships with Letters

What's the most likely initial 'greeting' you get in Retail Stores these days (assuming you get one at all?)

'Are you right?'

or,

'Can I help you?'

And your typical response to that last one is 'No thanks, I'm just looking'.

Happens all the time doesn't it?

But did you ever go into a store and have someone say something like this . . .

'Hello . . . thank you for dropping in'.

I bet you've never heard anything like it.

And yet if that happened, I'm also willing to bet you'd be impressed because it's so unusual. A 'thank you' is really rare isn't it? It's an often overlooked phrase. And yet such a powerful one.

In fact, it's such a powerful phrase that this entire Chapter is devoted to it. So that *you* become a 'thank you' giver.

You see, there are many opportunities for you to say 'thank you' and *build the relationship with your friends, customers, suppliers* and anyone who you deal with.

Here's a quick list of some of the things you can say 'thank you' for:

* An Order
* A Payment
* A Phone Call
* A Good Meeting
* A Letter
* For Being A Customer
* For Fixing a Problem That Needed Fixing
* For Being a Friend

Let's take the first one—thanking someone for buying.

Here's a typical example—where they took the time to say 'thank you'—trouble is they did it like they may have done it in England in the 19th Century.

Mr D Lamb
Tops Instant Printing
293 Howard Street
Sydney N.S.W. 2000.

Dear Mr Lamb,

Your valued order has been accepted and is being progressed to meet the required installation date.

I would like to take this opportunity of thanking you for placing your business with us, and to express the wish that our association will be long and mutually beneficial.

The PHONEMAN personnel who will be dealing with your requirements are listed below, please fell free to contact them with any queries you may have at any time.

Service & Installation Manager
MICK MUNRO

Client Liaison & Training
KATE SIMPSON

Administration & Accounts
CHRISTINE KELLY

Assuring you of our best attention at all times.

Yours sincerely,
PHONEMAN COMMUNICATIONS

Very formal isn't it? And full of onions.

So let's re-write it and see how much better it sounds:

Good morning David,

Congratulations once again for choosing PHONEMAN equipment.

I know you'll be delighted not just with the equipment itself, but by the way in which we continue to provide the type of service and support you'll be proud and happy to recommend to others.

> *Also David, it might be a good idea to take a note of the various people here who'll be dealing with. There's*

Mick Munro	*Service & Installation Manager*
Kate Simpson	*Training & Client Liaison*

and,

Christine Kelly	*Administration and Accounts*

These people and their staff are committed to making our association an excellent one.

David, your order is now being processed so that we'll be able to install the equipment on 7th March as promised.

Again, I'm delighted to be dealing with you David. We'll be working towards making our association a long and . . .

. . . . rewarding one

P.S. Kate will be in touch with you soon to arrange a suitable date to get the training underway.

That's far less formal. And as a direct result, the letter works better.

Most people don't take the time to say 'Thank You' for anything. You will have noticed how most people spend time catching people doing things wrong rather than doing things right.

Take for example, Accounts Department. Most times you only hear from them when you *haven't paid*. Or when they change their terms of trade. Like in this example, which does for communication, what Jack the Ripper did for blind dates...

MEMO TO OUR VALUED CUSTOMERS

Due to the ever increasing demand placed on our company for the collections of C.O.D's from your clients we have no alternative but to incur a surcharge of 20% on all C.O.D's collected with a maximum of $25.00 per C.O.D.

All C.O.D's shall be processed every Wednesday and cheques sent back by post that evening. All cash C.O.D's shall be returned the following day with the normal return charge being borne by the customer.

No claims against our company for non returns of C.O.D's shall be recognised unless lodged in writing within 14 days after the prior months invoice has been issued. These charges shall apply from Monday 8th September.

Assuring you of our best interests at all times as we head toward being one of the Nation's most stable and reliable transport companies.

And if you think that's bad, look at this one. (It is real—we didn't invent it.)

Dear Customer,

On reviewing your trading with us for the past six (6) months, it is obvious that you do not have an on-going need for our services. This being the case I will be with drawing your rates as of the 1st December and I have enclosed a schedule of our rates. If you have an unexpected need, it may be useful but you should be aware that as a non-account customer you would be charged twice the stated rates on the schedule.

Yours faithfully,

Sales Manager.

Instead of that type of stuff, wouldn't it be different to get a letter like this:

Good morning Mr Delmodes,

I'm not sure whether or not you get many letters like this one.

If you deal with others the way you deal with us, then you deserve *to get lots of letters like this.*

Let me explain. . .

> *You'll know that we sent you an account recently for your purchase of a set of office furniture. Nothing special about that I guess.*
>
> *Except this . . . you paid that account promptly—in fact a couple of days ahead of time. So, I'm just writing to say 'thank you' for that Mr Delmodes. We appreciate it very much.*

In fact, next time you're in the store, do drop by and say hello—I'd like to meet you personally.

Until then, do continue to enjoy . . .

. . . . good things

P.S. When you drop in I'd like to give you a small gift that you'll find very useful.

Different isn't it?

And what's Mr Delmodes encouraged to do? Keep on paying his accounts on time.

And think about the effect the letter generates in terms of word-of-mouth advertising . . . which is free advertising!

In fact, a Motor Dealer used that idea like this. He went to his Sales Manager and asked him if he'd had any people of influence invest in New Cars this month. If this new owner traded in a car as part payment on the new car, here's the kind of letter he'd receive from the Motor Dealer.

Good morning Mr Chandler,

You probably don't get many letters like this—letters that have real fifty dollar notes attached.

So I'd better explain. . .

I was talking recently with Bob Jones, one of our new car salespeople. (You'll recall Bob because he recently helped you select your new Commodore.)

When Bob quoted you a figure for your trade-in Mr Chandler, he thought we might have your vehicle in our showroom for some time.

We were wrong!

You see, your trade-in vehicle sold much quicker than we expected so we saved ourselves a little money—not much—but we did save money.

> *And when Bob told me about it he thought it would be a good idea to give you $50—in other words, he thought it would be good to let you have the benefit of that quicker sale.*
>
> *I agreed—so that's how come there's a $50 note attached for you.*
>
> *I'm not sure what you'll do with the $50, but I know you'll enjoy it.*

It's good to have you as a customer Mr Chandler. We'll be doing our best to continue to give you the kind of service and fairminded-ness so that you'll be happy to recommend to others. You can count on that.

Best regards,

. . . .

P.S. Nearly forgot! Congratulations for getting your new Commodore from us. When you drop in for your next service drop by my office—I'd like to meet you to say 'hello' and to make sure we're continuing to serve you well.

Again, think of the power of that letter generates in terms of free word-of-mouth advertising.

Now some people will say 'that's crazy—giving away $50 like that'.

Yet those same people would think nothing of running a $6000 ad in the newspaper. Perhaps an ad that screamed 'Do A Deal With Us'.

The $50 letter works.

And so does saying 'thank you'.

Perhaps the ultimate 'thank you' story concerns David Spencer.

He and his wife owned a Take-Away Chicken Store in a small Brisbane suburb. One November he called us to discuss doing 'a Christmas Special' in his store.

We decided to be different. In fact, we decided to give away a flower.

David ran a small newspaper ad with the headline **'Fancy Getting a Flower from a Chicken Store'**. He made an arrangement with a nearby florist to provide beautiful silk flowers to his customers.

When his customers came in just before Christmas he gave them each a silk flower with a hand-printed card.

Here's the card . . .

> *We just wanted to say 'Thank You'*
> *for being a customer*
>
> *Sincerely,*
> *David & Merrilyn Spencer*
>
> *P.S. Have a Happy Christmas.*

In three days David Spencer gave away 3000 flowers! And during January (4 weeks *after* his promotion) when most Australians leave for their holidays, David had record sales.

He was different. Because he found an effective way of saying 'Thank You'.

You see, what do many fast food stores do? They give you a free can of Coke. And how long do you remember the store? Until the last sip of Coke.

How long would you remember David Spencer's thank you card and flower?

I was presenting a Seminar 6 months later. I told the David Spencer story and a lady approached me during the break. 'I used to live in that area of Brisbane until I moved to Sydney,' she said. 'Guess what I've still got on my dressing table?'

You're right. She still had David Spencer's flower.

There's a message for you in that story—a message we sum up in our next Chapter. . .

Eleven

The Difference is You

If you had to pick a central theme for this book I guess the word 'different' would appear somewhere—taking a different approach, simply being different.

Simple ideas like changing 'Dear' into 'Good morning'. 'Yours faithfully' into 'enjoy . . . good things'. And simple ideas like WII-FM as the central core of every sentence.

Now whilst that might indeed be different, it is in fact. . . . . . you.

Let me explain. . .

Being 'different' means you need to view letter-writing differently. But in the past you've probably been taught to suppress originality and conform to a letter writing style that is outdated *and* ineffective.

So, please take *and use* the ideas in this book so that you can shake off conformity and become more creative.

> And on the subject of difference, we know that people buy the difference (or at least perceived difference) they see in products and ideas. They 'buy the difference' they see between you and your competitor in product sales, in job applications, in home loans or in any other area of activity.

And that raises an interesting point in the area of product sales.

You see studies show that the real differences between products are vanishing. The pace of change is so fast that it's now unlikely that you'll have a totally unique product. And with information now flowing so fast, if you do some unique thing today—your competitor copies it tomorrow.

> The reality is that never again will you have a long term product, service or price advantage. Because that's true (and because we know that people buy differences) then it leaves our buyer with little choice but to buy products or services based *on the people difference*.

In other words, in all situations whether they are business or personal ones, YOU (and not the product) are now the real difference. And **WRITE LANGUAGE** is all about making that difference become a reality.

Be yourself (your *real*) self in letters and you'll automatically be . . . different. You'll automatically have impact.

So we believe that we've not only given you some effective ideas but also the motivation and courage to use them.

You see, it doesn't take all that much effort to apply these ideas.

For example, to be different to your competitors and others (both in business and in your personal life)

THINK OUTSIDE THE BOX

Then, once you get used to the ideas, it becomes a habit pattern to

THINK IN WII-FM

Sure, it takes time to

CREATE A GREAT GOOD OPENING

but you'll be amazed how quickly you can create great openings once you start.

And then, because you're already *thinking* in WII-FM it's simple to:

CHANGE THOSE 'ONIONS' INTO EDIBLE MORSELS

by using

LINK PHRASES

Thinking about your reader makes it easy for you to use

INVOLVEMENT TECHNIQUES

From there, you'll see that

GREAT CLOSES

come easily too.

> These techniques are different. They *are* simple. And they work.

> They'll work for you too—*when you use them.*

Make a commitment to do that now. Make sure the next letter you write is YOU—make sure it's different. Make sure it's really communicating.

When you do that—when you use these ideas consistently—there's no doubt at all. You certainly will enjoy . . .

. . . writing letters that really work

ALLAN PEASE   **PAUL DUNN**

P.S. Nearly forgot! Thank *you* and congratulations for investing in the book.

Why not use Allan Pease as guest speaker for your next conference or seminar?

Pease International (Australia) Pty Ltd
Pease International (UK) Ltd

P.O. Box 1260
Buderim 4556
Queensland
AUSTRALIA

183 High Street
Henley in Arden
West Midlands
England, U.K. B95 5BA

Tel: ++61 (7) 5445 5600
Fax: ++61 (7) 5445 5688

Tel: ++44 (0) 1564 795000
Fax: ++44 (0) 1564 793053

Email: (Aust) info@peaseinternational.com
          (UK)   ukoffice@peaseinternational.com
Website: www.peaseinternational.com

Also by Allan Pease:

Video Programs
Body Language Series
Silent Signals
How to Make Appointments by Telephone
The Interview
Why Men Don't Listen and Women Can't Read Maps

Audio Cassette Programs
The Four Personality Styles
How to Make Appointments by Telephone
How to Remember Names, Faces & Lists
Why Men Don't Listen & Women Can't Read Maps
Questions Are The Answers
It's Not What you Say

Books
Body Language
Talk Language
Write Language
Questions are the Answers
Why Men Don't Listen and Women Can't Read Maps
Why Men Lie and Women Cry
Why Men Can Only Do One Thing At A Time & Women Never Stop Talking
The Rude & Politically Incorrect Joke Book

"WHY NOT USE ALLAN PEASE AS GUEST SPEAKER FOR YOUR NEXT CONFERENCE OR SEMINAR?"

**Contact Pease Training Corporation Pty Ltd.
Telephone (02) 973 1150 Fax (02) 973 1169**

Seminars conducted in over 30 countries

Also by Allan Pease:

VIDEO PROGRAMS
1) Body Language Series
2) How to Make Appointments by Telephone
3) The Interview
4) Silent Signals

AUDIO CASSETTE ALBUMS
1) The Body Language Workshop
2) The "Hot Button" Selling Workshop
3) The Four Personality Styles Workshop
4) How to Make Appointments by Telephone
5) How to Develop a Powerful Memory

BOOKS
1) Body Language
2) Talk Language (with Alan Garner)
3) Write Language (with Paul Dunn)
4) Memory Language (with Barbara Pease)

To:

**PEASE TRAINING CORPORATION
Box 350, AVALON BEACH, N.S.W. 2107
AUSTRALIA**

Please send me a catalogue of sales and management programs, and other material by Allan Pease.

Name ....

Address ....

....